what do we know and what should we do about...?

T0274343

slavery

Julia O'Connell Davidson

Los Angeles I London I New Delhi
Singapore I Washington DC I Melbourne

Los Angeles | London | New Delhi
Singapore | Washington DC | Melbourne

SAGE Publications Ltd
1 Oliver's Yard
55 City Road
London EC1Y 1SP

SAGE Publications Inc.
2455 Teller Road
Thousand Oaks, California 91320

SAGE Publications India Pvt Ltd
B 1/I 1 Mohan Cooperative Industrial Area
Mathura Road
New Delhi 110 044

SAGE Publications Asia-Pacific Pte Ltd
3 Church Street
#10-04 Samsung Hub
Singapore 049483

Editor: Natalie Aguilera
Editorial assistant: Rhoda Ola-Said
Production editor: Katherine Haw
Copyeditor: Catja Pafort
Marketing manager: Ruslana Khatagova
Cover design: Ginkhan Siam
Typeset by: KnowledgeWorks Global Ltd.

Library of Congress Control Number:
2021952258

British Library Cataloguing in Publication data

A catalogue record for this book is available from the British Library

ISBN 978-1-5297-3075-3
ISBN 978-1-5297-3076-0 (pbk)

contents

titles in the series

Forthcoming:

What Do We Know and What Should We Do About Terrorism?
Brooke Rogers

What Do We Know and What Should We Do About Sustainable Living?
Kate Burningham and Tim Jackson

about the series

Every news bulletin carries stories which relate in some way to the social sciences – most obviously politics, economics and sociology, but also, often, anthropology, business studies, security studies, criminology, geography and many others.

Yet despite the existence of large numbers of academics who research these subjects, relatively little of their work is known to the general public.

There are many reasons for that, but, arguably, it is that the kinds of formats that social scientists publish in, and the way in which they write, are simply not accessible to the general public.

The guiding theme of this series is to provide a format and a way of writing which addresses this problem. Each book in the series is concerned with a topic of widespread public interest, and each is written in a way which is readily understandable to the general reader with no particular background knowledge.

The authors are academics with an established reputation and a track record of research in the relevant subject. They provide an overview of the research knowledge about the subject, whether this be long-established or reporting the most recent findings, widely accepted or still controversial. Often in public debate there is a demand for greater clarity about the facts, and that is one of the things the books in this series provide.

However, in social sciences, facts are often disputed and subject to different interpretations. They do not always, or even often, 'speak for themselves'. The authors therefore strive to show the different interpretations or the key controversies about their topics, but without getting bogged down in arcane academic arguments.

Not only can there be disputes about facts but also there are almost invariably different views on what should follow from these facts. And, in any case, public debate requires more of academics than just to report facts; it is also necessary to make suggestions and recommendations about the implications of these facts.

Thus each volume also contains ideas about 'what we should do' within each topic area. These are based upon the authors' knowledge of the field but also, inevitably, upon their own views, values and preferences. Readers may not agree with them, but the intention is to provoke thought and well-informed debate.

Chris Grey, Series Editor

Professor of Organization Studies

Royal Holloway, University of London

about the author

Julia O'Connell Davidson is Professor of Social Research at the University of Bristol, UK. Her research has focused on economic life, including sex work, and how it is shaped by and reproduces inequalities of gender, race, class, age and nationality. She has also written extensively on the topic of "human trafficking and modern slavery", and currently holds a European Research Council award that examines what histories of enslaved people's efforts to move closer to freedom might teach us about the contemporary experience of marginalised and rightless groups, such as irregular migrants and asylum seekers.

1

introduction

In the eighteenth century, the highly profitable business of transporting kidnapped Africans across the Atlantic to be sold as "slaves" was lawful, as was "slavery" itself in the Americas. Most white Europeans and Americans regarded this state of affairs either as perfectly justifiable, or as a necessary evil. But towards the end of that century, the antislavery cause rapidly garnered popular and political support. The slave trade was outlawed by Denmark in 1803, by Britain in 1807, and by the United States in 1808. Slavery itself was legally abolished in Haiti in 1804 following the revolution that established the nation, and the nineteenth century subsequently witnessed its abolition throughout the Americas and across the British Empire. In 1948, Article 4 of the United Nations Universal Declaration of Human Rights banned slavery globally, and in 1981, Mauritania became the last country to abolish it in law. Yet in the twenty-first century, slavery is not merely a subject of historical interest. It is almost weekly in the news and a topic that inspires passionate concern. Why? What makes slavery into a "current affair"?

There are two different answers to this question, for slavery has been driven onto the current political agenda by two different sets of actors. For some activists, slavery is a pressing issue in the contemporary world because systems of domination set in train by Atlantic World slavery lived on post-abolition, and continue to generate gross inequalities globally and within nations. For others, slavery is a current affair because, although successfully abolished in the past, it has resurfaced and millions of children, women and men around the world are now victims of "modern slavery". While mainstream politicians and media commentators treat the first claim with scepticism and even outright hostility, the idea that "modern slavery" is an urgent global social problem has been readily accepted. In fact, it has established such a strong grip on the political and public imagination that eliminating "modern slavery" by 2030 is now included in Target 8.7 of the United Nations' Sustainable Development Goals (SDGs), and significant sums of money are available from governments and other funding bodies for projects and programmes addressing the issue.

To understand why the idea of "modern slavery" is so palatable to political elites, we need to go back to the 1990s, when there was growing political anxiety in liberal global north states about what came to be termed "transnational organized crime". In the context of more porous borders in the post-Cold War era, state actors were increasingly worried about the unauthorised cross-border movement of goods (especially drugs and guns) and people, which they bundled together as a threat to national sovereignty and security. The unauthorised movement of people was subdivided, however, into those migrants assumed to be complicit with the criminals, "smuggled persons", and those assumed to be their victims, "trafficked persons", who were at first typically imagined as women and children forced across borders and violently exploited in prostitution.

In 2000, the *United Nations Convention on Transnational Organised Crime* addressed these concerns, and was accompanied by supplementary protocols on both smuggling and trafficking (also one on arms). Where smuggling was said to be "a crime against the state", human trafficking was "a crime against the person" and so a human rights violation. Thus, although "trafficking" entered into international law as a problem of crime control not human rights, it was also discussed as a humanitarian issue. The idea of human trafficking as both a crime *and* an especially egregious violation of human rights was strengthened by extensive use of the metaphor of slavery by political leaders. George W. Bush, for instance, made reference to the transatlantic slave trade when explaining why the US should take a leading role in the global struggle against trafficking. The history of Atlantic World slavery was also frequently invoked in political rhetoric surrounding the introduction of the UK's Modern Slavery Act (2015) that increases the penalties for trafficking offences, and that of similar legislation enacted in Australia, the Netherlands, and France.

This rhetoric, and the term "modern slavery" itself, bore the strong imprint of a new brand of antislavery activism that emerged towards the end of the twentieth century and popularised the idea that trafficking is the modern-day equivalent of the transatlantic slave trade: the process by which human beings are transported into slavery. It also propagated the idea that in the twenty-first century, slavery takes many different forms, including forced labour, "forced marriage", debt bondage, the worst forms of child labour, domestic servitude, enforced criminal activity, organ trading, child soldiers, and more. Until the late 1990s, the long established, British-based organisation Anti-Slavery International had been the main NGO in the field. But at this point, the idea of "modern slavery" as a scourge of our times started to be heavily promoted by new NGOs based in affluent, global north countries, often Christian faith-based, and with a good deal of money and political influence.

The International Justice Mission, a US non-profit established in 1994 is a case in point. After receiving a US State Department grant of over $700,000 in 2002 to implement measures against "sex trafficking" in Thailand, it received $9.8 million from Google in 2011 to lead a coalition fighting slavery in India, and by 2015, its year-end net assets were $20.03 million. Free the Slaves, another US-based non-profit, was founded in 2000 and now annually generates between $2 and 3 million in contributions. Cable Network News (CNN), a US-based multinational pay television channel with an estimated net worth of $5 billion, established the CNN Freedom Project in 2011, while the charity Walk Free was founded in 2012 by Andrew and Grace Forrest. Andrew Forrest is an Australian mining magnate with an assessed personal net worth of about A$27 billion. In the same period, many more NGOs, small and large, were established to fight trafficking and "modern slavery", while numerous existing NGOs concerned with various rights violations reframed the problems they address as "modern slavery" since this had become the hot humanitarian topic of the early twenty-first century.

The many NGOs now active in the field of antislavery are diverse in certain respects. Some adhere to a deeply socially conservative and religious world view, others are informed by more secular humanist beliefs. Some focus on garnering popular support for the antislavery movement and use extremely simplistic sound bites and catch phrases to do so, others focus on influencing international policy debate and use more sophisticated language and arguments. But all share a vision of slavery as antithetical to the existing liberal capitalist world order, and hence something that can be tackled without overthrowing or radically transforming that order. Indeed, many of the "big players" hold that freedom is a foundational value of liberalism, and free wage labour is fundamental to capitalism as an economic system. Slavery is an anomaly in a world that is largely ordered by liberal principles and institutions, and economically powered by capitalist enterprise, and this is precisely why antislavery NGOs are confident that "modern slavery" can be eliminated and its estimated 40 million victims can be liberated.

Though found in many and disparate situations, "modern slaves" share a common exposure to exceptional violence and degradation, antislavery NGOs tell us. They are treated as mere objects and possessions, and subjected to extreme exploitation from which they cannot freely walk away. In poor global south countries, the problem is linked to the absence of the rule of law and slow or uneven economic development. In the global north, "modern slavery" is concealed within a criminal underworld. Though this makes it tough to tackle, we can look forward to a slave-free world in the not too distant future, providing that governments commit to promoting economic development and strengthening liberal institutions around the world; that laws against slavery are strengthened and law enforcers trained to enforce them; and that businesses, civil society organisations and the general public work together to root out "modern slavery" in all its forms. This is not an agenda that ruffles feathers in the global north. People from across the mainstream political spectrum are happy to endorse it.

However, slavery is also currently in the news for reasons that do not generate the same comfortable consensus. In 2020, the brutal police murder of George Floyd in Minneapolis, USA, ignited a wave of Black Lives Matter (BLM) protests around the world, and shone a spotlight on a very different way of understanding of slavery as a contemporary social issue. For decades, Black radical and critical race theorists and activists have been arguing that the racial inequality, violence and oppression set in place by Atlantic World slavery was not erased by the legal abolition of slavery, but remains an ongoing social problem. Transatlantic slavery was foundational to the development of the modern social and political order in Europe and the Americas, and its racial logic continues to underpin the privileges enjoyed by people racialised as white, and the multiple vectors of exclusion, discrimination and inequality faced daily by people racialised as Black, which include, but extend well beyond, police brutality and racism in the criminal justice system.

This logic also informs the way in which the history of liberal societies is popularly imagined, taught and represented, scholars and activists argue. The murderous violence used to appropriate the labour, land and resources necessary for the development of modern capitalist economies is whitewashed out, and replaced by a story about beneficent, liberty-loving heroes freeing the slaves and civilising benighted savages. The fact that there are still memorials celebrating individuals who orchestrated and enriched themselves through transatlantic slavery in civic spaces is regarded as one expression, albeit figurative, of the continuing lack of value attached to Black lives. Hence, during a Black Lives Matter (BLM) demonstration in the city of Bristol in June 2020, protesters tore down a statue commemorating the philanthropy of Edward Colston, a seventeenth century merchant who derived a significant part of his immense wealth from slave trading. They flung the statue into the city's harbour from which the slave ships that helped to enrich Colston once set sail.

The BLM movement experienced something of a #MeToo moment around the world in the spring of 2020, but popular and political reactions to BLM protests, including the direct action to remove Colston's statue, were not unanimously positive. Some actively denounced them. And where mainstream media coverage simply accepts and reproduces Antislavery NGOs' claims about "modern slavery", it presents critical analysis of the Afterlives of Atlantic World slavery as "controversial". Politicians who unambiguously decry "the scourge of modern slavery" are also more circumspect about making statements or symbolic gestures in support of BLM activism. Indeed, in the UK in October 2020, Kemi Badenoch, women and equalities minister, went so far as to say that it is unlawful for schools to teach certain elements of critical race theory as fact. Moreover, partly in response to the toppling of Colston's statue, a new Police, Crime, Sentencing and Courts Bill introduced by the UK government in March 2021 included measures to increase the maximum penalty for criminal damage to a memorial from three months to ten years.

There are, then, two very different perspectives on what makes slavery an urgent contemporary problem and on what we should do about it. One generates calls for civil society organisations to join hands with liberal states to combat the crime of "modern slavery". The other demands that liberal states are held to account for the system of slavery they historically sanctioned and benefited from, and for their continuing devaluation and disregard for Black lives. This book reviews both perspectives. After providing some brief historical background on Atlantic World slavery and the similarities and differences between the experience of enslaved people and formally free servants and wage labourers in the past, it turns to what we know about "modern slavery" and about the "Afterlives of slavery". The "What do we know?" section examines the forms of exploitation and violence experienced by wives, workers, migrants and criminalised and stigmatised groups such as sex workers that contemporary antislavery NGOs discuss under the heading of "modern slavery". It then considers "Afterlives" thinking on how laws, policies and practices in the post-abolition world re-enshrined forms of exclusion, violence and inequality that had been foundational to slavery in such a way as to allow them to reach into the contemporary moment. The "What should we do?" section then reviews the very different programmes for action generated by the analyses offered by "modern slavery" and "Afterlives" thinkers.

The book argues that though each approach is grounded in a concern with human flourishing and freedom, the "modern slavery" perspective rests on an analysis that is readily co-opted by state actors and powerful elites that have no interest in changing the current status quo. By contrast, the "Afterlives of slavery" perspective challenges existing structural and systemic inequalities and injustices. If fulfilled, the demands for change articulated by "Afterlives" scholars and activists would not only help to ensure that Black lives matter, but also go a long way towards addressing the situation of those described as victims of, or vulnerable to, "modern slavery".

background

There is no neutral, apolitical story about the history of Atlantic World slavery and its abolition. Popular histories in Europe and North America assert that transatlantic slavery was the relic of a benighted age that ended with the spread of liberal political ideas and the development of industrial capitalism. Through this lens, the story of the development of liberal global north societies appears as one of incremental progress towards freedom. British history, for example, is often told as a proud story that moves from a "dark age" in which vassals and serfs were denied rights and freedoms to the "Age of Enlightenment" that ushered in the liberties "we" now take for granted. The story sometimes acknowledges that Britain played a part in the transatlantic slave trade and tolerated slavery in its colonies, but emphasises its role in the legal abolition of slave trading and slavery in the nineteenth century, and applauds the foresight, humanity and grit of white Britons, men such as William Wilberforce and Thomas Clarkson, who campaigned for abolition.

The fact that the British government took on substantial debt to fund compensation payments to slave holders for the loss of their "property" under the Slave Compensation Act of 1837 typically goes unremarked. Yet UK taxpayers continued to service this debt until 2015, and this is one of many ways in which the legacies of colonial slavery 'reach into the present' (UCL, 2022). It means that the author of this book, and almost all its UK readers, have helped, however briefly, to enrich slaveholders and their descendants.

In other European countries and in the United States, acts of abolition and proclamations of emancipation are also popularly represented as completing a historical progression towards liberal modernity and freedom. In this celebratory narrative about the history of liberal societies, freedom is imagined as the absence of physical force. Liberating the mass of ordinary people from the shackles that bound them to kings, lords, masters, or slaveholders is also understood as a pre-requisite for the development of a modern industrial capitalist economy. Capitalist economic activity is not planned and directed by an elite group using brute force to impose their will on their political subordinates, but rather driven by a multiplicity of mutually beneficial, contractual market exchanges of goods for money and labour for wages. For capitalism to thrive, all must be free to sell their labour or the products of their labour to the highest bidder. Only then can the "invisible hand" of the market work to perform its wonders. Political equality and market freedom go hand in hand, and today's liberal capitalist democratic societies represent the end point of developmental progress towards human freedom.

This is the political worldview that informs the thinking of many of the NGOs at the helm of the contemporary movement against "modern slavery". However, this version of history is contested by a great deal of scholarship. As shown below, historical evidence does not lend support to the idea of a sharp line between pre-modern and modern social orders, or of a necessary relationship between modern liberal capitalism and universal freedom. Capitalist development was made possible by the violent expulsion of independent peasants from their subsistence land, as well as the violence of colonialism and slavery, and capitalist enterprises exploited the labour of a diverse mix of free and unfree workers. The working and living conditions of formally free servants and workers often overlapped with those endured by the enslaved. Atlantic World slavery was integral to, rather than incompatible with, the development of capitalist modernity. What distinguished it both from previous forms of slavery and from systems of formally free wage labour, many scholars argue, was its *racial* logic, a logic that continues to disfigure contemporary societies and the global political and economic order.

Atlantic World slavery: A very brief history

Different forms of slavery are known to have existed in prehistoric communities and to have been present historically in most regions of the world.

For thousands of years and through to the twentieth century, in many human societies around the world "slave" was one of a number of social statuses that defined and structured relationships between human beings. Use of the term "slavery" to evoke maltreatment, injustice and tyranny has an almost equally long history. The ancient Greeks, and later the Romans, used slavery as a metaphor to describe the condition of freeborn male citizens who were tyrannised by a political despot. But whilst objecting to the fact that *they*, freeborn men, were being treated as if they were slaves, they considered it quite acceptable to enslave people who fell into the category Aristotle termed "natural slaves". These were beings with incomplete souls who lacked intelligence. Like domesticated animals, they needed a master to guide and direct them.

People defeated in war were also often imagined as deserving of enslavement. From the fourth century, for instance, Christian theology taught that captives taken in a just war could legitimately be enslaved. Indeed, some argue that the stigma associated with enslavement is grounded in slavery's origins in war. Those taken captive in battle were sometimes offered a choice between being put to death, or slavery. If they accepted the humiliation of slavery over death, they were dishonoured by that "choice". This helps to explain why "slave" has also historically been used as an insult, and why "slavish" is still a derogatory term for behaviour regarded as fawning, servile, or unimaginative. The idea of slavery as a debasing form of dependency is also present in talk of being "a slave" to passion, drugs or alcohol. In the past, "slave" worked as an insult because it was understood to reference a being without dignity, rights or honour, a being that *did* deserve to be enslaved.

Chattel slavery, and the stigma that attached to it, persisted for centuries after the fall of the Roman Empire in some parts of Europe. The Mediterranean slave trade, for example, ran from the twelfth to fifteenth centuries and mostly involved Venetian and Genoese merchants who supplied sugar-producing Crusader states with enslaved Slavs from the Dalmatian Coast. As this trade declined, the Portuguese started transporting people from West Africa into slavery in Madeira and Cape Verde where they were developing sugar production. Although the Portuguese and Spanish enslaved local inhabitants when they initially began to colonise the Americas (as did the English and French when they later established their first colonies), they also developed this trade in enslaved people from West Africa to provide labour for their colonial ventures. That trade grew to become the first Atlantic system, followed in the seventeenth and eighteenth centuries by the second and much larger system, dominated by English, French and Dutch traders and investors.

The ubiquity of slavery throughout human history makes it easy to imagine that Atlantic World slavery was simply the continuation of an archaic practice, a vestige of more barbarous, pre-modern times. But was it? It is certainly true that when the transatlantic slave trade developed in the early sixteenth century, it was rooted in older traditions of raiding, ransom and enslavement still or recently practised at the time by Europeans and North Africans as well as in other parts of the world. However, the 400 year long system that subsequently developed was distinctive from all that had gone before in several very significant respects, which together suggest that slavery was not only perfectly compatible with, but integral to, the development of liberal modernity. First, the transatlantic trade was distinguished by its immense magnitude. Estimates vary, but the Transatlantic Slave Trade Database, the largest repository of information about the trade, originally created by historian David Eltis in 1999 and developed and updated since, puts the number of people forcibly shipped from Africa to the Americas at approximately 12.5 million, with around 1.8 million dying during the "middle passage". Many more are known to have died whilst en route to, or being held in, slaving ports in Africa.

Second, as philosopher Charles Mills (1997) observed, transatlantic slavery appeared and flourished alongside the development of liberal Enlightenment thinking on questions of rights and freedom, and the exploitation of enslaved people in the Americas actually intensified through the eighteenth and much of the nineteenth century. In other words, Atlantic World slavery thrived in the period *following* the English industrial revolution and the French and American revolutions, events that are usually taken to mark the historical transition to "modernity", and during the period when capitalism developed and expanded to become the globally dominant economic system.

The labour power of enslaved Africans and their descendants was brutally exploited in a wide range of economic activities in the Americas, generating the wealth and supplying the raw materials necessary to the development of industrial capitalism in Britain and other European countries as well as northern states of the USA. Furthermore, slavery's efficacy as a system of both political domination and labour exploitation in the nineteenth century rested heavily on the kind of bureaucratic and organisational strategies that are widely regarded as modern (inventories, accounting practices, surveillance technologies, task and bonus systems of labour control and discipline, and so on). Indeed, some "modern management" techniques that came to inform assembly line production in the twentieth century were first developed and trialled on slave plantations in the US South (Rosenthal, 2018). For all these reasons, Atlantic World slavery was *modern* slavery, and not merely the vestige of an archaic social practice. This fact is easier to grasp when considered alongside the historical evidence showing the very partial, contingent and tenuous relationship between freedom and liberal capitalist modernity.

Capitalism and free wage labour

Capitalism is generally thought of as an economic system that brings capital (in the form of factories, machinery, raw materials, etc.) together with free wage labour in a production process that creates profit. Profits are reinvested in capital to produce further profits, and in this way wealth is generated. Yet history shows that far from depending exclusively on what would today be considered as "free" workers, modern capitalist economies developed and thrived on a diverse mix of forms of unfree and semi-free workers, as well as those who conformed to the ideal-type of the "free" wage labourer and those who were legally ascribed slave status. Coercion and violence were initially features of capitalist development because the labour force required by a capitalist economy did not simply exist historically, ready in waiting for capitalist employers to provide jobs in factories, mines, fields and so on. A class of people who depended on wage labour had to be created.

In Britain, this process began in the fifteenth and sixteenth centuries with the "enclosures". Land that had till then provided ordinary people with access to the common resources they depended upon for food, fuel, bedding, and shelter was taken into private ownership, a process that continued into the late nineteenth century. Initially, there was not enough paid work to absorb all those thrown off the land. Those who wandered the country in search of other means of survival were viewed by elites as a serious threat to the established social order. They were criminalised as "vagabonds" and "vagrants", and punished with whipping, stocking, branding, ear cropping, and execution. In the seventeenth century, Poor Laws added to the legal armoury that controlled the mobility of the poor and coerced them into wage labour. It was only towards the end of the eighteenth century that anything resembling a free market in labour was allowed to develop. Even then, it was closely hemmed in by vagrancy legislation that continued to immobilise the poor and keep them in their geographic and social "place" by criminalising a wide range of informal earning activities, as well as "idleness". The criminalisation of hunting and fishing as "poaching" further restricted opportunities for the poor to fend for themselves without waged work. Those convicted under such laws faced severe punishments, including transportation into forced labour in the colonies.

There was a system of poor-relief for those who could not find paid work, but in 1834, it was reformed such that applicants were forced to enter workhouses to secure it. On admission to the workhouse, husbands were separated from wives, children from parents. They were effectively imprisoned, subject to forced labour, half-starved, and disciplined by means of violence. Even workers fortunate enough to find a buyer for their labour power were not always paid enough to protect themselves and their dependents from starvation. Malnutrition, lack of clean water and sanitation, pollution, damp and squalid housing all contributed to the misery of workers in English industrial towns, where mortality rates soared in the 1830s and 1840s, and protesters described the absence of state intervention to ameliorate their situation as "social murder".

The capacity of the poor to sustain life was now determined by nothing more than market forces. When they found paid work, the relations surrounding their employment were a far cry from what today is understood by the term "free wage labour". In Europe and America until towards the end of the nineteenth century, labourers were allocated one of a number of statuses (apprentices, journeymen, labourers, servants, "industrial immigrants", and so on), each of which bound them to their masters to varying degrees by a legal machinery that set the limits of the freedoms that "free" workers (and masters) enjoyed. The freedom to quit an employment relationship was one of the key aspects of freedom that was differentially limited by such laws. In seventeenth century England and its American colonies, the law locked most workers into lengthy relationships with their masters and those who left before their term had expired were treated as "runaways" and risked imprisonment. In Britain's American colonies in the eighteenth century, the profitable trades of importing both servants and slaves boomed in response to perceived labour shortages, and an internal market for bound workers, as well as slaves, developed. "Free" servants, as well as slaves, were rented out, sold, and hunted as fugitives by their masters if they ran away.

In the US, it was not until the nineteenth century that indentured servitude came to be viewed as an illegitimate restriction on individual freedom, and even then, legally sanctioned systems of wage forfeiture still sometimes operated to lock workers, especially migrant contract labour, into dependency on their employers. In England and in Canada, Masters and Servants' legislation, which covered factory workers as well as agricultural and domestic workers, and which made worker absence, desertion, insubordination, and unsatisfactory work punishable by imprisonment, was not repealed until the 1870s. After that, it continued to apply in British colonies, where well into the twentieth century it provided whipping, as well as imprisonment, as the punishment for formally free servants guilty of absence or misbehaviour. All in all, the history of employment relations in liberal capitalist societies reveals significant overlaps between slavery and other systems designed to establish and maintain hierarchies of domination and servility. But there were also important differences between slavery and wage labour as systems of domination.

Atlantic World slavery as racial slavery

Atlantic World slavery differed from previous forms of slavery in terms of its scale, organising principles and enmeshment in a modern, global economic system. It also differed with respect to the question of *who* was enslaved and the rationale for their enslavement. Previously, slavery had variously been regarded a substitute for death in war, a punishment for certain crimes, a means of repaying debt, a condition of birth, or was justified on religious grounds. The latter did also play a role in the transatlantic system, but there was slippage between religious and "racial" thinking from the start, with Portuguese navigators and merchants using the term *"negro"* (Black) interchangeably with that of slave. Over the centuries of Atlantic World slavery, both freedom and slavery came increasingly to be imagined in racial terms. Though there were differences between the race thinking that developed in different parts of the Americas, in general, whiteness became the colour of uncontested freedom and citizenship, while Blackness was increasingly associated with chattel slavery and imbued with its profound and dehumanising stigma.

Atlantic World slavery was not only "modern slavery", then, but also *racial* slavery. This is important to understanding its distinct legal architecture, and so also to recognising why and how the experience of the enslaved and that of "free" servants and labourers diverged.

The legal architecture of racial slavery

Dictionaries tell us that the slave is "a person who is the legal property of another and is forced to obey them" (Oxford); or "a person legally owned by another and having no freedom of action or right to property" (Collins). The definition of slavery offered in international law by the 1926 League of Nations' *Slavery Convention* also approaches it as a property relation: slavery is "the status of a person over whom all or any of the rights attaching to ownership are exercised". For liberal thinkers, this is what makes slavery uniquely abhorrent. In 1845, George Bourne, one of the founders of the American Anti-Slavery Society, described the singular wrong of slavery as the fact it makes "free agents, chattels – converting *persons* into *things* ... uncreating A MAN to make room for *a thing!*" (pp. 7–8).

It is certainly true that in the Atlantic World, the enslaved were legally constructed as objects of property, and a precise specification of their monetary worth could be made for purposes of market exchange, mortgaging, taxation, insurance, and the valuation of estates. They could be and were bought, sold, bequeathed, wagered, gifted, and rented out. At moments of exchange and accounting, they were represented in the manner of "things". Though servants could also be bought and sold in early colonial times, their servitude was always time-limited. Slavery was, as a rule, a lifelong condition. Moreover, unlike servitude, slavery was hereditary, with the legal doctrine of *partus sequitur ventrem* ruling that the status of children born to enslaved women followed that of their mother.

It is also true that in many contexts and at many times, enslaved people were beaten and worked to death in a fashion that resembled in certain respects the treatment of oxen or donkeys. But enslavement did not literally turn human beings into objects or brutes. Nor, in fact, were slaveholders interested in purchasing and owning enslaved people as mere bodies or things. They wanted to exploit them as humans, with all that this implied in terms of the capacity to reason, plan, react, collaborate, create, and move. The problem for slaveholders, however, was that the human qualities that made the enslaved potentially valuable as workers could also be used by the enslaved themselves to escape, resist, or act collectively to overthrow the conditions under which they were constructed as objects of commodity exchange and property ownership.

Because enslaved people were conscious, purposive, human actors, not "things", slaveholders were (to varying degrees according to time and place as well as the individual slaveholder's circumstances) dependent on the state to enforce their power over slaves. The criminal law was a central means by which slave states met this challenge. Unlike the livestock to which they were routinely compared, enslaved people in the Atlantic world were arrested, tried, and punished for committing outlawed acts. Criminalised acts included all forms of refusal to submit to the authority of a legal owner or any white person, any act of resistance against their violence, and any effort to escape. Slaveholders' power over the enslaved was thus backed by a wider system of terror emplaced by slave codes and the punishments they provided, which made the alternative to compliance truly horrifying.

Slaveholders' enjoyment of their rights in enslaved people as property or "things" was made possible by a legal edifice that controlled the enslaved as criminally culpable *persons* (Patterson, 1982). Thus, rather than being characterised only by its treatment of human beings as objects of property, Atlantic World slavery was a system of domination that gave the enslaved a dual life in law, as both things *and* persons – or rather sub-persons. The legal structure that states built to wall people into the prison of slavery also extended beyond this. It criminalised acts of solidarity, compassion or care on the part of people of free status, both white and Black. Harbouring or otherwise assisting escapees from slavery was illegal. In various places at various times, white men – whether slaveholders or not – were legally obliged to administer a whipping to enslaved people found wandering without a pass to prove they had permission to move from their enslaver. In some places, it was unlawful to teach enslaved people to read. Slaveholders' rights to grant freedom (manumission) to their human property was also often heavily restricted in law, and many slave codes decreed that slaveholders should not allow their human property to act as if they were free.

Slavery was not simply a relationship between enslaved individuals and the slaveholders who had legal rights of possession over them, then. Slave status also designated a particular, degraded and inferiorised relationship to the state and the law. The economic value of slaves both on the auction block and in processes of productive and reproductive labour was underwritten by state violence and its threat. Slavery in the Americas involved more than the reduction of human beings to objects of trade. It required the construction of complex legal and political machineries that institutionalised a power hierarchy by creating and enforcing slavery as a permanent, hereditary, inferior and dependent status. And because Atlantic World slavery was racial slavery, these machineries built white dominion over those racialised as Black into the political structures and logic of the modern era. This is what gives modern, racial slavery its lasting and corrosive significance. Abolishing the laws that allowed for ownership of human beings as chattel did not automatically overturn the laws that, in various ways and to varying degrees across the Americas, enshrined a racial hierarchy in terms of rights and freedoms.

what do we know about slavery?

"Modern slavery"

Antislavery NGOs' websites and campaigning materials tell us that although chattel slavery has been legally abolished around the world, slavery persists in a variety of forms and there are some 40.3 million "modern slaves" across the globe today. A majority of those affected are women and children, but adult men also fall victim to "modern slavery". And, they say, where Atlantic World slavery victimised people racialised as Black, today's slavery is "colour-blind", with slavers preying on the weak and impoverished regardless of their race. No nation is immune. Campaigners provide examples that span an array of otherwise very different phenomena in very different contexts and settings. We are told, for instance, that in the global south, "modern slavery" includes brick kiln and brothel workers bonded to their employers by debts they can never repay; children working in extremely hazardous conditions or forced into early and abusive marriages; and migrants sold into slavery by their traffickers. Around the world, there are migrant workers confined and abused by employers who have confiscated their passports to prevent their escape.

Global north nationals are also said to be at risk. Teenage runaways who get trafficked into sex work; homeless people or people with learning difficulties who are forced to work long hours on farms or tarmacking roads; and children coerced into drug dealing, pick-pocketing, shoplifting or other criminal activities, are all included under the umbrella of "modern slavery". Antislavery NGOs stress that "modern slavery" is a uniquely terrible wrong. "This is not about lousy marriages, this is not about jobs that suck", says Kevin Bales, a leading antislavery figure, in his TedX talk (2010), "I'm talking about *real* slavery". To reinforce that message, campaigners highlight cases in which people have suffered extreme, often gruesome, violence at the hands of their exploiters when discussing these examples.

Contemporary antislavery campaigners see themselves as continuing the struggle of the original antislavery activists of the eighteenth and nineteenth centuries. But there is a crucial difference between then and now. Historically, although Atlantic World slavery made a key contribution to the development of the modern, liberal capitalist world order, it also existed as a separate and particular system for extracting and exploiting labour, and a separate and particular system for creating an exploitable class of aliens or sub-persons. This made the object of the original antislavery cause clear and straightforward. Antislavery activists were not attempting to remedy every evil in their world, but specifically to bring down the system of chattel slavery. They could (and some did) say something along lines of: "We recognise that many free servants and wage workers/wives/child labourers prisoners/workhouse inmates suffer appalling abuse and exploitation, and this should be addressed. However, *we* are concerned to end the particular wrong of slavery." They could then target their efforts on liberating those who were legally ascribed the status "slave", leaving other activists and reformers to address the injustices faced by other groups.

Today's antislavery campaigners aspire to do the same. As the NGO Free the Slaves puts it: "Free the Slaves believes that all labor abuses and human rights abuses are wrong. Our mission, however, is ending slavery" (www.freetheslaves.net). But does slavery still exist as a bounded and distinct phenomenon that can be addressed independently of other labour or human rights abuses? And if so, how do we identify the slaves that must be freed? Contemporary antislavery actors state that today, slavery has three defining elements. First, "modern slaves" are controlled through violence or its threat, or psychological coercion; second, they have lost "free will" and free movement; and third, their exploitation is so severe that they are paid nothing, or nothing beyond subsistence. To qualify as a "modern slave", you must be forced into an exploitative situation and prevented from exiting it by another person or persons. Or as Bales and Soodalter (2009: 13) put it, "When we aren't sure if someone is, in fact, a slave, we can ask one basic question: 'Can this person walk away?'"

The Walk Free Foundation's *Global Slavery Index* (GSI) is the source of the widely cited 40.3 million "modern slaves" figure. The GSI relies in part on survey data Walk Free gathers in a sample of countries around the world. The screening questions employed in the survey to identify potential victims of "modern slavery" all centre on the use of force. Respondents are asked, for example, whether they have "ever been forced to work by an employer or a recruiter?" or "ever been forced to marry?" Again, the questions reflect an understanding of "modern slavery" as an umbrella term for crimes (and/or practices that campaigners believe should be criminalised) in which physical force or its threat, or "psychological coercion", is used to compel people to perform labour, marry, or take part in criminalised activities such as marijuana cultivation, benefit fraud, or shoplifting.

Boundary troubles

One problem with the three-element definition of slavery is that it does not allow for clear-cut, indisputable determinations of whether someone is a "modern slave". In the past, before slavery was outlawed, the question of who was and who was not "a slave" was straightforward. "Slave" was a status given in law. It did not have to be deciphered from elements of each individual's lived experience. People ascribed slave status were slaves, whether or not they experienced the three things that antislavery actors say are constitutive of slavery today, i.e., force, restriction, and exploitation. In fact, historical evidence shows that, though rare, there were people who had slave status in law but did not actually experience any of those three things. There were, for instance, some whose legal owners allowed them to live as if free, and/or who managed and controlled the labour of other enslaved people – the story of Anna Jai Kingsley, who was transported into slavery in Florida and later became a slaveholder provides one remarkable example (Schafer, 2018). Equally, as has been seen, there were many formally free servants, wives, workhouse inmates and so on who *did* experience all the individual elements taken by contemporary antislavery actors to constitute slavery, but were not ascribed slave status in law.

We are told that today "modern slaves" are distinguished by the fact they experience force, restriction, and exploitation, yet none of these three things are absolute, either/or conditions, and none of them are exceptional.

Indeed they are features of all our everyday lives. We all know, for example, that if we tried to waltz through an airport without showing our passports, violence or its threat would very quickly be used to prevent us from so doing; that we cannot just stop making payments on our mortgages or loans without facing serious penalties; and in most cases that our employers reap greater financial rewards from our labour power than we ourselves do. Violence, restrictions on free choice and movement, and exploitation range along a series of intersecting continuums, from those that are minimal through to those that are extreme.

Matters are complicated further by the fact that some very heavy restrictions on freedom are lawful and socially tolerated. People who join the British army aged over 18, for instance, cannot quit whenever they please, but are bound to their employer for the duration of their contract under threat of imprisonment (up to 2 years in military prison if they go Absent Without Leave in peace time, and up to a maximum penalty of life imprisonment for those who abscond after being given an order to deploy in war). They are not free to "walk away", but few would describe them as victims of "modern slavery".

The grim litany of violence and abuse highlighted in antislavery campaigning materials should appal anyone who reads it. But by insisting that "modern slavery" is a unique and distinct problem that can be tackled independently of other labour and human rights abuses, Antislavery NGOs deflect attention from the systemic and structural factors that actually generate both the kinds of violence and exploitation that concern them, and the abuses they say fall beyond their remit. I will illustrate the problem first by looking briefly at marriage and women's rights, then turn to labour abuses that are (and are not) discussed under the heading of "modern slavery".

"Modern slavery", marriage, and women's rights

Until the mid-nineteenth century in the US and the late nineteenth century in Britain, the common law doctrine of coverture suspended the separate legal existence of women on marriage. It was the husband who, as head of household, enjoyed the status of civil citizenship, and until the enactment of Married Women's Property Acts, white wives, like chattel slaves of America's Southern states, could own nothing, possess nothing, acquire nothing in their own right. From Mary Wollstonecraft on, there were white feminists who likened marriage to slavery, and remained critical of it even after women secured formal legal equality in Europe and North America.

Today's antislavery NGOs are not opposed to marriage *per se* (indeed evangelical Christian antislavery NGOs are firmly in favour of it), but they do identify forced, servile, and early marriage as forms of "modern slavery". Campaigning materials often present the latter as a "cultural problem" that affects women and girls in "traditional" societies of the global south, and ethnic minority women in liberal global north countries, and highlight shocking practices, such as bride kidnapping in rural Kyrgyzstan, said to affect as many as 12,000 women each year. Consent is used to mark the moral boundary between the "good" marriage on the one hand, and all forms of slavery-like marriage on the other. In its "International pledge to commit to making the ending of forced marriage a global priority", Walk Free invited people to sign up to the statement: "I believe marriage should be a partnership between two consenting adults. That no man, woman or child should ever be forced, bullied, sold or trapped into a marriage" (www.walkfree.org).

Yet the line between forced marriages and those that are entered voluntarily does not necessarily correspond to a line between "bad" coercive, violent and exploitative relations and "good" equal, consenting partnerships. Even when women consent to marriage as a contract, rather than being forced into it, that contract can initiate the power relations that make violence and exploitation possible. In fact, in many parts of the world, marriage still changes a woman's legal standing in such a way as to resemble the historical standing of people with slave status in the Atlantic World. In Northern Nigeria, for instance, women live under a tripartite legal system consisting of statutory, customary, and sharia laws, and the Penal Code grants husbands permission to beat their wives for the purpose of correction, providing the violence does not result in "grievous hurt". There are no sanctions against marital rape; wives need their husbands' permission to obtain a passport or to travel outside the country; and male heads of household generally control decisions regarding property (O'Connell Davidson, 2015).

In Qatar, a male guardianship system legally restricts women's freedom of movement and choice, and forces them to obtain permission from their male guardian to marry, study abroad on government scholarships, travel abroad until certain ages, and receive some forms of reproductive health care. As Human Rights Watch (2021) observe, the power and control given to men by this system fosters and fuels violence, and leaves women with few viable escape options. The version of the guardi-anship system that operates in Saudi Arabia has recently been reformed, but women still require the permission of a male relative to obtain a divorce. If we asked Bales and Soodalter's (2009) diagnostic question of Northern Nigerian, Qatari or Saudi wives in general, not just victims of forced marriage, we would surely have to conclude they are victims of "modern slavery".

This problem is not limited to countries where the law forces women into dependency on husbands and male relatives. In the UK, women are no longer legally constructed as wards of their husbands and are in theory offered legal protection against violence. Yet huge social, psy-chological, financial and legal barriers to escaping abusive relationships remain, especially for poorer women. Such barriers have been strength-ened by legislation that makes it harder for women to access the legal aid necessary to be able to walk away from a violent and exploitative husband or partner. They are higher still for migrant women whose immigration status is dependent on maintaining a relationship with the husband or partner. Immigration regulations that impose a "spousal pro-bationary period" of five years leave migrant spouses in a very vulner-able position in relation to the partners or spouses who sponsor their entry and right to remain.

Measures to combat forced marriage do not address the fact that women around the world who *do* give full and free consent to marriage or cohabiting partnerships can nonetheless end up exploited, controlled by violence or its threat, and unable to freely leave the relationship. To imagine a world in which women were *really* free to walk away (and so a world in which practices such as bride kidnap, abduction, sale, and other direct physical coercion of women and girls into marriage were rendered pointless), we would have to imagine a world in which women – both citi-zen and migrant – enjoy full and equal access to the means of life, educa-tion, housing, social protection from the market; full and equal access to mobility, justice, divorce, contraception, abortion, and child care. A world in which relations between men and women are no longer conceived as naturally hierarchical.

Women's vulnerability to forced marriage, like their vulnerability to being trapped in marriages that range from lousy through violent to deadly, is produced by the patriarchal laws and social structures that to a greater or lesser degree force women into dependence on men. Calling forced marriage "modern slavery" deflects attention from this, and allows us to forget that, to the extent that women in some parts of the world are currently freed from such dependency, that freedom has been won through feminist political struggle, not antislavery activism.

Labour abuse and "modern slavery"

The workers who feature in Antislavery NGO campaigning materials as victims of "modern slavery" are mostly either informal sector workers, or international migrants, or both. The term "informal sector" is generally used to refer to small economic units within which labour relations do not usually rest on contractual arrangements with formal guarantees, but are casual and often based on kinship or personal and social relations. Such units are found in many sectors of the global south, including manufacturing, brick kilns, construction, agriculture and Artisanal and Small Mining (ASM), but are also present in global north economies. According to the International Labour Organization (ILO), about 2 billion workers, or 60 per cent of the world's employed population ages 15–64, spend at least part of their time in the informal sector (cited in IMF, 2021: 10).

The labour of informal workers is vital to the global economy. For example, in 2020 some 44 million people in the global south were reliant on ASM (Artisanal and Small-scale Mining) for their livelihoods. These informal workers extract, pre-process and trade high value commodities such as cobalt, mica, and tungsten, used to produce the consumer items, medical equipment and electric vehicles central to everyday life in affluent global north societies, as well as essential materials for construction projects around the world, and also precious stones and gold (World Bank, 2020). Many global south informal sector workers are internal migrants, but international migrants are also found working in the informal sector in both global south and north countries.

The labour of international migrant workers is also critical to the functioning of the global economy. The ILO estimates that in 2019, there were some 169 million international migrant workers, and two-thirds of them work in high-income countries. In many regions, they form a significant portion of the labour force and make a vital contribution to key economic sectors and the provision of essential services such as health and social care and transportation. Among international migrant workers, there are people who are classed as "highly skilled", earn very good money and enjoy a fairly elite lifestyle. But many more undertake precarious "3-D" jobs (dirty, difficult, dangerous). Though some enter destination countries through irregular channels and work in the informal sector, others arrive legally, often with temporary migrant labour or "guest worker" visas to work in specific jobs. For many countries, their labour is the lifeblood of sectors such as agriculture, forestry, seafood processing, construction and more.

While both informal sector workers and international migrant workers make crucial contributions to the contemporary global economy, they are also known to commonly experience terrible working conditions, very low pay, and to be vulnerable to a host of labour abuses. In ASM, for instance, occupational hazards include respiratory diseases, silicosis, tuberculosis, arthritis and in some cases also mercury poisoning. Workers usually labour without proper equipment or safety gear and there are many major and minor accidents due to blasting, falls, and landslides. Living, as well as working, conditions are usually appalling. Workers often live in makeshift temporary housing, without sanitation or access to clean drinking water, without electricity, or health services or educational facilities for children. Most brick kiln workers in South Asia face equally dreadful conditions. Meanwhile, in small manufacturing plants and sweatshops across the global south, workers toil in cramped and airless conditions, without adequate protection from dust, machinery or fire, sometimes in buildings at risk of collapse.

The many thousands of migrants who pick fruit and vegetables across the EU and the UK (some of whom are legally present on the territory and others not), also frequently live in squalid makeshift camps and labour for long hours in appalling conditions for well below the minimum wage. Their access to paid work is often mediated by gangmasters who take a sizeable cut of their wages, and also claw back wages by charging high fees for transportation, accommodation, even drinking water supplied during the days spent working in blistering heat.

The Gulf Cooperation Council (GCC) states are heavily dependent on migrant labour, especially for construction, hospitality and domestic work. Indeed, the region is one of the main destinations for migrant workers and the proportion of migrant to local workers is one of the highest in the world. Reports of labour abuses of various types are rife, and over the past decade, the condition of migrant construction workers present in Qatar as it prepares for the World Cup have been very much in the media spotlight.

Around 6,500 of these workers are estimated to have died between 2011 and 2021 as a result of the atrocious conditions in which they live and work, and some have been violently assaulted when they complain (Pattison and McIntyre, 2021).

In some cases, employers and/or recruiters also impose heavy restrictions on informal sector workers' freedoms and/or use violence against them. Horrific cases have been documented in India, for example, of employers who rape women and girls in families employed in ASM and brick kilns, and who beat, even in some instances maim or kill, workers who attempt to quit (ASI, 2015). There is also evidence that some employers manipulate the debts accrued by informal workers in such a way as to make them impossible to ever repay, so that they and their families have no choice but to continue to labour for mere subsistence for many years. In some parts of South Asia, the debt can even pass from one generation to the next. Likewise, many shocking cases involving the false imprisonment, rape and even torture and murder of migrant workers are well evidenced (see, for example, ILO, 2013; IOM, 2019).

Antislavery campaigners do not claim that every informal sector worker or every migrant worker is a "modern slave" but as with marriage, limit their concern to situations where they believe consent is absent. This reflects an implicit and highly questionable assumption that workers are divisible into those who in principle enjoy the liberal liberty to enter and retract from contracts, and "modern slaves" who do not. Antislavery NGOs often seek to free the latter in order that they may join the former. For instance, in a 2012 TEDx talk, when American photographer Lisa Kristine recounts the story of her work in the global south with Free the Slaves, she includes an anecdote about a group of debt-bonded South Asian ASM workers that the NGO helped to escape their creditor and secure a quarry lease of their own. "Now", she tells us, "they do the same backbreaking work, but they do it for themselves, and they get paid for it, and they do it in freedom".

The emphasis on consent leads Antislavery NGOs to care in a very selective way about informal sector and international migrant workers. In the absence of meaningful alternatives, people will consent to and remain in all manner of contracts, including extremely harmful and exploitative ones. Workers who perform the most hazardous labour in the worst circumstances have not necessarily been forced into it. The deadly conditions for construction workers in the Gulf have been widely publicised in the countries that supply migrant workers, for example, yet people still queue up outside recruitment offices hoping for a chance of a job there. Likewise, despite knowing all too well the risks of artisanal mining, when the authorities shut down informal mines, ASM workers often vigorously protest.

When the alternatives are grim enough, people will not only consent to extremely hazardous work but also to jobs that pay next to nothing. Informal sector employment sometimes generates relatively good earnings, but many workers earn only enough for daily survival. It is therefore very easy for "freely consenting" workers to become trapped in a cycle of poverty or mired in debt. Moreover, in some regions, especially those affected by conflict, all workers can be targets of violence from armed groups and public and private security forces, as is the case for ASM workers in the Democratic Republic of Congo. Meanwhile, sexual harassment and exploitation can be a feature of women workers' experience whether or not they have freely chosen the work and could freely retract from it.

There is no doubt that the world would be a better place if somehow, overnight, every worker who is currently under the violent control of an employer, creditor or recruiter was released from their grip, and antislavery actors' ambition to achieve this may look progressive. But it looks less progressive if we recognise that workers who are free from such violence can still end up "choosing" backbreaking work in conditions that may kill them, still face violence from other actors, and still do not necessarily earn enough to do more than subsist without falling into debt. Indeed, "freeing the slaves" without addressing other forms of labour abuse and transforming the structures and systems that leave people vulnerable to violence and unable to walk away from highly exploitative, degrading and/or dangerous situations looks something like trying to place a sticking plaster over a gaping gunshot wound.

There is no separate and distinct system of slavery that leaves informal and international migrant workers vulnerable to the kinds of violence and exploitation of concern to antislavery actors. Rather, that vulnerability, like vulnerability to more general labour abuses, is inextricably linked to the systems and structures that support contemporary global capitalism, and/or the systems that nation states use to monopolise their control over the international movement of people, and to criminalise particular populations.

Neoliberal capitalism, labour abuses, and "modern slavery"

In the nineteenth and twentieth centuries, labour reformers and activists engaged in political struggles against labour abuses. Among other things, they argued that labour is life itself, not a commodity, and fought to secure rights that would protect the human worth of workers. Their aim was to "de-commodify" labour, and prevent employers from simply sucking dry and discarding workers as they might any other piece of merchandise. European and American labour activists successfully secured legislation on issues such as working hours and the right to join unions. Towards the end of the nineteenth century, the laissez-faire liberalism that had thus far shaped the meaning of "free wage labour" began to give way to a regime that placed certain restrictions on (some) employers' freedom to do as they pleased in their relations with (some) workers.

The organised labour movement gained strength in the twentieth century, and helped shape the political settlement that became the norm in welfare capitalist states in the post World War II period. That settlement entailed state interventions to provide social security payments and public services that, to a greater or lesser degree, shielded individuals and families from total dependence on wage labour for their survival. Welfare capitalist states also intervened to moderate employers' treatment of workers, introducing policies that afforded (some) workers certain rights pertaining to health and safety, sickness, retirement, and unfair dismissal.

By the 1970s, organised labour had secured a regime within which free wage labour for most white, male worker citizens in global north countries no longer looked anything like slavery. They typically enjoyed relatively stable employment in relatively good working conditions, and state welfare provisions ensured that they and their families had access to basic education, health care, housing, unemployment benefits, sick pay and pensions. Such workers therefore enjoyed a high level of freedom to walk away from any employer who maltreated them. Governments of many newly independent former colonies sought to emplace a similar model. Even though they lacked the resources to provide the same level of welfare to their citizens, they nonetheless helped to improve the lot of rural and urban populations, and often unions secured better working conditions and wages for those employed by foreign owned as well as national and nationalised companies.

Then came the global economic crisis provoked by the 1973 oil price shock, swiftly followed by the rise of right wing, free market politics in affluent global north countries. There were sustained political efforts to dismantle the gains that organised labour had secured in the post-war period. Unions came under attack, welfare spending was cut, public services and nationalised industries privatised, and the regulations that had previously constrained those who owned and controlled capital were loosened. In the emerging global regime of neoliberal capitalism, capital was increasingly concentrated in the hands of large transnational corporations (TNCs) that were able to shift manufacturing production out of global north countries to cheaper locations in the global south. Here, they could access workers who, without access to adequate welfare and social protection, had little choice but to accept harsher conditions and low wages.

Though the service sector expanded in the global north, the jobs it provided were more precarious. These trends have continued, supported by new digital technologies that have allowed for the development of "gig economies", such that today, precarious freelance, temporary and zero hours contract employment, as well as informal sector work, is increasingly common in the UK, Canada and the US.

Debt, dispossession and labour exploitation

In the global south, the 1970s economic crisis generated a debt crisis. It dramatically increased the costs of imports, throwing newly independent states into recession and rapidly increasing governments' foreign debts as they sought loans from the International Monetary Fund (IMF) and World Bank. When US dollar interest rates rose at the start of the 1980s, debt repayments skyrocketed to consume huge swathes of government revenue. Across the global south, the IMF and World Bank made loans conditional on the enactment of harsh austerity measures and economic restructuring. Indeed, the structural adjustment packages (SAPs) tied to such loans have been characterised by some as a war against the poor and a form of neo-colonialism.

Throughout the 1980s and 90s, SAPs undermined traditional forms of subsistence economies, encouraged the growth of industries producing raw materials and commodities for export, redirected subsidies away from social spending and basic commodities towards debt servicing, involved massive currency depreciations and a concomitant drop in the price of labour, and provoked high unemployment. Until the 1970s, agrarian and land redistribution policies implemented by a number of global south governments were gradually decreasing the land inequality that derived from histories of colonialism. But from the 1980s, land inequality started to increase again as a result of large-scale industrial farming models supported by market-led policies and other neoliberal reforms.

Alongside this, the reduction or elimination of agricultural subsidies left small farmers unable to compete in global markets and the landless people who once relied on them for waged work found themselves unable to survive in rural areas. The new millennium brought no relief. Indeed, the global financial crisis of 2007–8 resulted in an intensification of land-grabbing as countries dependent on food imports (Korea, Japan, Saudi Arabia, for example) sought to outsource food production to fertile farmland in countries such as Uganda, Sudan, Pakistan, and Cambodia. This, alongside growing markets for biofuels, made agricultural land into a strategic asset for international investors looking for new strategies for growth, and both corporations and states have acquired millions of hectares of farmland, also forests and peatlands.

As a result, rural communities have found themselves dispossessed of their traditional means of subsistence. Members of workless and displaced rural communities (often drawn from communities already marginalised and stigmatised on the basis of caste or ethnicity) therefore move in search of paid work. The opportunities available to them are mostly in informal worksites discussed above. Such worksites have proliferated partly as a consequence of the growing market power of TNCs. In the context of neoliberal economic reforms and deregulation of markets, TNCs have been able to adopt a business model that allows them to parcel risks and costs down to their suppliers. This model has led to a "race to the bottom" as suppliers compete to provide TNCs with goods and components at ever lower prices. Suppliers achieve this by subcontracting elements of production out along increasingly complicated supply chains that ultimately lead to small, informal and often extremely dangerous worksites and sweatshops.

The association between this model and a variety of forms of labour abuse is well known. In the 1990s, a series of exposés revealed the presence of child labour in the supply chains of a number of household name brands, including Nike, Reebok and Marks & Spencer. Most TNCs have subsequently paid much greater attention to their public relations, yet they have also continued to pursue the same basic business model, using their vast market power to drive costs down. For instance, between 2014 and 2018, Finland's biggest grocery retailer, the S Group (which operates 1,800 retail outlets and reported 2018 revenue of €11.5 billion), negotiated a 15 per cent fall in prices paid to suppliers of tomato products in Italy. Italy's big tomato processors passed these cuts down to farmers supplying raw tomatoes. This, along with similar cuts by other huge TNCs that buy canned tomatoes, incentivised suppliers to exploit migrant tomato farm workers more intensively (Oxfam, 2019).

As this example shows, the practices of TNCs affect workers in global north as well as global south countries, a fact borne out by many recent scandals, from revelations in 2020 about severe exploitation in multinational Tyson Foods' poultry plants in the US, to those about the conditions of workers in Boohoo's clothing sweatshops in the UK. Very often, the workers affected are international migrants.

State control over mobility: Citizen and migrant workers

Neoliberal economic reforms have also contributed to many people's decisions to migrate internationally for work and provided debtor governments with a strong economic interest in their citizens' labour emigration. Remittances from migrants increasingly substitute for the social welfare that global south states are no longer unable to provide. As noted above, the majority of labour migrants undertake "3-D" jobs. Indeed, migrants have long been socially imagined as cheap and biddable workers, willing to accept pay and conditions that would be refused by citizen workers. Yet such differences as do exist between migrant and local workforces in this respect are created by states, in much the same way that historically, the differences between enslaved and free workers were created by state and law.

Contemporary states claim a right to determine whether or not to admit foreigners on their territory, and on what terms. They assign a variety of different legal statuses to migrants that set varying limits on their rights and freedoms, including their freedoms in relation to the labour market. Countries that depend heavily on migrant labour typically provide aspiring migrants only with temporary authorisation to work in the destination country. Depending on the country and on the particular type of work permit they are issued, a variety of further restrictions on workers' rights and freedoms are imposed. Some countries attach conditions to work permits that deny migrant workers the right to marry, or engage in "immoral or undesirable" activities, or even to become pregnant. Migrant women employed in industries such as footwear and garments in Malaysia, for example, must undergo mandatory pregnancy testing prior to departure and annually thereafter, and are deported at their own expense if discovered to be pregnant (Fair Labor Association, 2018).

More commonly, authorised labour migrants may be prevented from bringing their children and partners into the country, even when this implies years of family separation; they may be legally denied rights to join trade unions, and excluded from employment legislation that provides other workers rights and protections. Even when they are not formally refused the right to unionize, other restrictions imposed on temporary migrant workers' freedoms can make it extremely hard for them to organise collectively (Anderson, 2013). All such measures heighten the risk of abuse and exploitation, even for those migrants who are legally present as workers.

One of the main ways states try to ensure that admittance onto their territory will not allow temporary migrant workers to claim the freedoms that citizens enjoy is by ensuring that their immigration status bonds them in various ways to the employer who sponsors them. The *kafala* system that brings temporary migrant workers to the GCC states and Lebanon provides one example. Migrant workers, like those in Qatar mentioned earlier, can only enter when sponsored by an employer to whom they are bound for the duration of the contract. The *kafala* system is notorious for the powers it grants sponsoring employers over their foreign workers, who cannot move to another employer or leave the country without their permission. Over the years, there have been many reports of violence, exploitation, and other abuse by sponsors under the *kafala* system, and Antislavery NGOs have supported other human rights and trade unions' campaigns for its reform.

However, temporary or "guest" worker visas in numerous other countries also legally tie workers to the employers who sponsor their entry and deny them freedom to move within the labour market. Such visas, which are the norm rather than the exception, force workers into dependency on the sponsoring employer. They, too, are frequently associated with abuses such as housing workers in insanitary conditions, requiring them to work long hours, overcharging them for housing, telephone and other services, and sometimes cheating them of wages. Whether enacted in the European Union, Australia, or the United States, in Singapore, Malaysia, or Thailand, the objective of temporary work visas is to ensure that migrants' labour power is available for the benefit of employers and the national economy, while simultaneously preventing migrant workers from securing the rights, benefits and protections available to worker citizens. Or, we could say, such measures are designed to allow the temporary migrant worker's labour power to be bought and consumed as a "thing", without also having to acknowledge that worker as a "person".

These immigration rules undermine the bargaining power of migrant workers, making them into a cheap and disposable workforce for "good" employers, as well as leaving them with inadequate protection against "bad" employers. They also open up extremely lucrative markets for the services of recruitment and placement agencies, both legal and criminalised. These politically constructed markets turn vast numbers of migrants, not an exceptional minority, into debtors.

Labour migration and debt

The fees charged for brokering legal migration are exorbitant. Officially sanctioned recruitment fees in some countries are equivalent to four or five months' salary, and it is legal to withhold a substantial portion of wages pending the worker's return home. When coupled with compound interest on loans advanced to pay them, legal as well as illegal charges can leave migrants seriously indebted. Debt is an often insurmountable obstacle to quitting and returning home, even when the debt is not to the employer, but to a money-lender, a family member, or a recruitment agent back home (or all three). Given the role that it plays in the UK's criminal justice and immigration detention systems, it is worth noting that British security company G4S has recently been embroiled in a scandal concerning its recruitment practices. An investigation revealed that migrant workers from south Asia and east Africa have been forced to pay illegal fees to recruitment agents to secure jobs as security guards for G4S in the United Arab Emirates (Pattisson, 2021).

Antislavery NGOs are concerned with the situation of migrants whose employers use force or its threat to prevent them from quitting, calling them victims of "modern slavery". But given the above, employers themselves do not need to use violence to prevent temporary migrant workers from challenging or quitting exploitative and dangerous conditions. The immigration rules that tie them to a sponsor and deny them free movement in the labour market, as well as the debts that are a routine feature of migration, in themselves constitute a significant barrier to being able to freely walk away from an unwanted or abusive employment relation. As well as creating vulnerability to abuse by mandating some migrants' dependency on a sponsor (an employer or spouse), immigration regimes force others into different types of dependency by making their movement and stay "illegal".

Illegality, dependence, and violence

The transatlantic slave trade relied on overwhelming physical force at every stage of movement. Antislavery NGOs describe human trafficking as a "modern-day slave trade". Yet today, the irregular migrants who end up in highly exploitative and heavily restricted conditions – like those whose journeys lead to more positive outcomes – are invariably people who actively want to migrate. They also generally have excellent reasons for wishing to do so. In fact, if we are looking for a historical comparison, they have more in common with people who sought to flee *from* Atlantic World slavery than those transported *into* it. Certainly, the measures that have been enacted by states in Europe, North America and Australia since the 1990s to keep them out look very much like high-tech versions of the techniques designed by slave states to keep enslaved people in.

Today, there are razor wire fences, and drones, as well as armed patrols that monitor borders. Slave states fined sea captains who help fugitives escape; today there are carrier sanctions against ships and planes that transport passengers without proper documents. Surveillance systems that combine radar, cameras, and X-ray technology are used to scan commercial trucks at ports. The use of thermal imaging cameras at ports in France, Belgium and the Netherlands has encouraged migrants and refugees to stow away in lorries with refrigerated containers where scanners cannot so easily detect the heat of bodies. However, the risk of suffocation is far greater, as was the case for the 39 Vietnamese people tragically found dead in a lorry in Essex in 2020.

State efforts to prevent border crossings also make journeys more dangerous by pushing migrants to take longer and more perilous routes through deserts or by sea. Border controls also encourage dependence on third parties who are better equipped to navigate them. It is true that some of those who facilitate unauthorised migration rapaciously exploit migrants' and refugees' need or desire to move, charging huge amounts of money for extremely risky journeys. Some cheat would-be migrants, some are violent, and some even continue to brutalise and exploit the migrants they promised to assist after arrival in the destination country. But many more provide the service they promised, even if for an exorbitant fee, and some offer assistance for entirely altruistic reasons (Sanchez, 2015).

Again, dependency leads to a continuum of experience but states treat everyone who offers help to people on the move without state authorisation in the same way. As slave states historically criminalised those who assisted fugitive slaves, so contemporary EU states criminalise humanitarian acts to preserve the lives of migrants and refugees. Between 2014 and 2019, more than 250 Europeans and Britons, mostly in Greece, Italy, Denmark, France, Germany, Spain, and the UK, were arrested, charged or investigated under various immigration laws for providing humanitarian assistance to migrants and refugees (Archer et al., 2019). The list, which continues to grow, includes fire fighters and ship captains who have assisted drowning people, and priests, politicians and humanitarian actors who have provided food, shelter, transport and other support to migrants. In September 2021, the former mayor of an Italian town who welcomed and assisted migrants and refugees was given a 13 year prison sentence for abetting illegal migration and irregularities in managing asylum seekers.

Migrants and asylum seekers are themselves being punished under such laws with equal or greater brutality. In Greece, a Somalian asylum seeker who took the wheel of a boat foundering on the Aegean sea in an effort to save himself and 33 others aboard was sentenced to a total of 142 years in prison by the Greek authorities in 2021, while a Syrian refugee is serving a 52-year term for crossing from Turkey with his wife and three children. The bereaved father of a 6-year-old child who died during their attempt to cross from Turkey to the island of Samos is being prosecuted for child endangerment. In the UK, 19 asylum seekers who steered, or assisted in steering, small boats across the Channel were jailed between June 2020 and 2021, for terms between 16 months and four-and-a-half years.

Border violence

Since it began recording in 2014, the Missing Migrants Project (2021) has documented the deaths of almost 3,000 people who died trying to cross the border from Mexico into the United States. The organisation UNITED for Intercultural Action has documented the deaths of more than 40,555 refugees and migrants between 1993 and 2020 attributable to the restrictive immigration policies of the EU (UNITED, 2020). In some cases, especially in "push back" operations, state actors are directly responsible for deaths.

In 2020, EU member states used illegal operations to push back at least 40,000 asylum seekers from Europe's borders, using methods that led to the death of more than 2,000 people (Tondo, 2021). Documenting illegal pushbacks in the western Balkans, the Border Violence Monitoring Network (2021) found abuse and disproportionate force was present in nearly 90 per cent of testimonies, including examples of migrants being whipped, robbed, stripped naked and sexually abused by members of the Croatian police. Reports of equally appalling violence by US border patrol officers are also commonplace.

State-sponsored violence against migrants and asylum seekers does not end here. The UK is one of the largest users of immigration detention in Europe, caging around 24,000 people a year under Immigration Act powers. Since detention is an administrative process, not a criminal procedure, migrants and refugees are detained at the decision of an immigration official, not a court or a judge, and there is no time limit on immigration detention in the UK. There have been a number of exposés revealing detention staff subjecting detainees to racist abuse and physical and psychological violence.

One detention facility featured in a Panorama exposé in 2017 was run by the private security firm, G4S (mentioned earlier in relation to its illegal recruitment practices for its UAE operations). G4S has made £2 million per year from operating this centre alone. Its Home Office contract stipulates various "performance" issues that can lead to deductions from its fees. The value attaching the lives of inmates is well illustrated by the fact that these include a paltry deduction of £10,000 if someone dies following self-harm, in contrast to a £30,000 deduction if an inmate succeeds in escaping (Corporate Watch, 2019).

The picture is similarly grim in the US, where the numbers of people affected are far greater. Every day, around 52,500 people are incarcerated by Immigration and Customs Enforcement (ICE) in more than 200 detention centres (Walia, 2021). The most well known scandal involves the fact that in 2019, the US caged a record 69,500 migrant children, at least seven of whom died whilst in state custody. But there are also less widely publicised reports of cases of asylum seekers being choked, beaten, pepper-sprayed and threatened with more violence to make them sign their own deportation papers, and of sexual violence against women detainees. To this grisly list of people who have been deprived of liberty and subject to a range of cruelties by state actors we could add the more than 4,000 people who were held against their wills, sometimes for years, in offshore hellholes such as Nauru and Manus Island by the Australian government.

The big players in the antislavery movement have had very little to say about any of the above. They do, however, apply the term "modern slavery" to the horrific experience of many thousands of refugees from Eritrea, Somalia and Sudan, as well as people migrating from sub-Saharan Africa towards Europe, who have been held hostage and ransomed or taken captive and subject to forced labour in the Sinai, Libya and elsewhere. Yet even this phenomenon is not a stand-alone problem connected to any traditional or new system of slavery. It is inextricably linked to migration policies being pursued by the EU. From the 2000s, the EU began externalizing its immigration control and Schengen border enforcement to "buffer states", using its political and economic power to encourage non-EU neighbours (especially North and West African states) to undertake certain control functions to suppress irregular migration on their behalf (Andersson, 2014). This has included financing migrant holding and "processing" camps in Libya and other countries known to have terrifying records with regard to the violation of migrants' human rights.

These measures are designed to immobilise peaceable men, women, and children who are doing nothing more than seeking to escape violence and/or other threats to their lives and wellbeing, or to realise dreams and ambitions that young people from global north countries take for granted their right to pursue. By immobilising them in extremely politically and economically unstable regions, the EU makes them vulnerable to victimisation by both criminals and state actors. In addition to the thousands who have drowned in the Mediterranean, or been tortured for ransom, many thousands more have been held captive in detention centres and prisons in unbearable conditions, beaten, whipped, raped, hung, starved, subject to forced labour, murdered, or deported and dumped in the Sahara desert without water or food.

Similar policies are being pursued by the US in Central America with similar effects. To be sure, the private and state actors who violently exploit the misfortune of the immobilised are morally repugnant. But the EU and US policy-makers who push irregular migrants and asylum seekers into their hands through policies that prioritise keeping fellow human beings out of their territory over keeping them alive and safe are certainly equally despicable.

Criminalisation and "modern slavery"

Over the past decade in the UK, as in many other global north countries, there has been growing criminalisation of every aspect of the lives of people who enter the territory without state authorisation, or who arrive through legal channels but overstay or otherwise break the terms of their visas (including temporary migrant workers who escaped an abusive relationship with the employer who sponsored their visa). Hostile environment policies mean they cannot lawfully work, rent a home, access medical care or education, or open a bank account. Those who assist them in accessing any of these necessities are also criminalised. People who are legally present and seeking asylum are prohibited from undertaking paid employment, even though the financial support to which they are entitled is so paltry (a mere £39.63 per week at the time of writing) as to make daily life unbearable, and they are often housed in squalid, damp and overcrowded accommodation. This penury can last for years, as the backlog of asylum cases currently runs to almost 71,000.

When asylum cases are rejected, it takes resources, support and courage to appeal the decision (and over half of such appeals find grounds to overturn the decision to reject). Many rejected asylum seekers end up in a situation of forced destitution, or are taken into detention. The new Nationality and Borders Bill aims to make it a criminal offence for an asylum seeker to arrive in the UK without authorisation, a law that will criminalise the vast majority of asylum seekers.

Those who are legally constructed as rightless aliens must depend on others to mediate their access to the means of life. Relationships between asylum seekers and irregular migrants and people who help them survive vary widely. In some cases, the person who assists is a relative, friend or sympathetic acquaintance who offers support as an act of solidarity or care. If they provide access to paid work, they exercise no control over the work pattern or earnings. In others, it is more like a regular (though criminalised) employment relation, where the third party directs the worker's labour and pays a wage.

Unsurprisingly, those denied the right to work and rent are often willing to accept jobs that pay well below the minimum wage, and to enter into arrangements whereby an employer or creditor provides them with accommodation and subsistence in lieu of wages. Such arrangements are not necessarily associated with violence or its threat, and even when financially exploitative, they may be regarded by the worker concerned as far better than the alternative, namely being destitute and sleeping rough, or being detained and forcibly removed to a place they do not wish to go. Their legally constructed and heavy dependency on third parties to access the means of life also makes them vulnerable to exploitation by unscrupulous employers who know that they will not dare report wage theft, sexual harassment or violence for fear of detention and deportation.

Cases of the latter are identified by antislavery NGOs as a form of "modern slavery", and this has given a veneer of humanitarian concern to immigration and police raids on informal workplaces such as hand car washes, takeaway restaurants and brothels in the UK. Yet the reality is that only a tiny minority of migrant workers found in any given worksite are considered by law enforcers to reach the threshold of victimhood required to count as a "victim of trafficking" or "slave". For the workers affected, a raid means being rounded up and aggressively interrogated by Immigration Compliance and Enforcement (ICE) officers. Sometimes, their fingerprints are taken using mobile scanners, and/or the officers search the premises for documents and driving licenses, in order to be able to prosecute irregular migrants for the crime of driving while "illegal". They may then be arrested and taken to the ICE base, where private security guards will hold them captive.

From here, they may be released with reporting requirements, or transported to a detention centre, where they may be held for weeks, months or in some cases, years. Ironically, those held in detention *are* permitted to undertake certain forms of paid work for the (often privately run) detention centre, for which they are paid well below the minimum wage. Migrants and asylum seekers know only too well what the likely outcomes of such raids are. In one tragic case in Newport in 2018, a young asylum seeker died during a police and immigration raid on a car wash when he fell from a roof he had scaled in his panic to escape.

Non-migrant slaves

In most global north countries, it is not only the lives of irregular migrants and asylum seekers that have become harder in recent years. Austerity-driven cuts to welfare and public services for young people, the homeless, those with mental health or drug problems, victims of domestic violence and so on, have negatively affected poor and marginalised groups of nationals, and the criminal law has also increasingly been used against them. In the US, laws criminalizing homelessness have increased since 2011, and many cities have introduced bans on virtually all life-sustaining activities undertaken by homeless people, from "loitering" to begging, to sleeping in public or in vehicles, to storing belongings in public.

In the UK, the Anti-Social Behaviour Crime and Policing Act (2014) equips local councils with powers to use Public Space Protection Orders to criminalise particular, non-criminal, activities taking place within a spec-ified area. These powers are being used to prosecute homeless people for begging and for rough sleeping, as well as to criminalise young people for "loitering" or engaging in any form of activity deemed "antisocial", and to "disperse" women involved in street sex work. NGOs that support people with mental health problems and learning difficulties in Australia, the US and the UK have expressed concerns about the growing criminalisation and incarceration of these groups.

At the same time as being increasingly constructed as "criminals", the same groups are also now represented as vulnerable to trafficking and "modern slavery". Indeed, the UK's National Referral Mechanism, set up in 2009 to locate and identify "potential victims of trafficking" (VoTs), annu-ally identifies more nationals as potential victims than it does migrants. UK nationals are also much more likely to be officially recognised VoTs or "modern slaves", and afforded the paltry rights and benefits that go along with that status than are migrants.

The kind of activities that have been re-labelled as "modern slavery" are not new, and mostly involve one or more people taking advantage of the vulnerability of socially and economically marginalised individuals who are young, and/or have learning disabilities, mental health problems or addictions, or are experiencing homelessness, in order to exploit them in some way. Clearly, this kind of exploitation is wrong and deeply unpleasant. However, a wealthy society that tolerates both homelessness and the criminal law being used against people who sleep rough or beg, and in which around 34 per cent of the prison population has a learning difficulty or disability (Prison Reform Trust, 2019) hardly seems in a position to pass moral judgment.

Sex work

Sex workers also deserve special mention in any discussion of the relationship between criminalisation and trafficking and "modern slavery". In most countries of the world, sex workers have traditionally been viewed as part of a threatening, dishonourable, criminal underclass, and are often routinely harassed and abused by police officers as well as members of the general public. As Amnesty International (2016a) has noted, whether in Norway, Hong Kong, Papua New Guinea or Argentina, "sex workers are without the protection of the law, and suffering awful human rights abuses". Research in Jamaica, the Dominican Republic, and the US has also shown that police violence is an everyday feature of sex workers' lives. At the same time as being widely criminalised, sex workers also frequently appear as victims of trafficking and "modern slavery" in NGO, media and political commentary on the topic. Indeed, some religious as well as radical feminist thinkers consider that all women in sex work are by definition victims and slaves, since they cannot imagine that any woman would consent to sell sexual services.

There is now a very large body of independent academic research on the sex sector (e.g., Kempadoo et al., 2005; Mai, 2018; Skilbrei and Spanger, 2019) which points to the conclusion that the vast majority of both national and migrant sex workers choose this form of work, albeit often as the best of a poor bunch of options. For those who migrate internationally, sex work abroad promises higher earnings than sex work or any other form of work available to them at home. It therefore promises the chance to remit money home to support dependants and/or to save lump sums that will enable them to set up businesses on their return, or to further other life projects.

Again, tighter border controls have made travel more difficult and expensive, and so increased dependence on third parties who can help to finance or facilitate unauthorised movement. In some cases, the risk of being refused entry at the border is a factor that encourages sex workers to enter into a form of indentured labour with an employer in the destination country. If the employer pays their travel costs upfront with a view to them paying the debt off through sex work on arrival, it is the employer not the worker who takes the financial hit if border control officers deny them entry and send them home.

Whether international migrants or not, some sex workers work independently, and others enter into a variety of employment relationships with third parties who directly or indirectly organise their labour. Relationships with such third parties vary along a continuum rather than leading to a neat either/or division between those who are "free" and those who are "enslaved". Within this, the people who fall victim to violence and exploitation extreme enough to be regarded by the authorities as "victims of trafficking" or "modern slaves" are very few in number. This means that police and immigration raids on sites of sex work are as unwelcome to most sex workers as are raids on other informal sector workplaces to other informal sector workers.

What do we know about the "Afterlives" of Atlantic World slavery?

In 2013, three radical Black organisers in the United States – Alicia Garza, Patrisse Cullors, and Opal Tometi – initiated a movement building project in response to the acquittal of the man who killed unarmed 17-year-old Trayvon Martin in 2012. They named the movement Black Lives Matter, and describe it as "an ideological and political intervention in a world where Black lives are systematically and intentionally targeted for demise". The Black Lives Matter (BLM) project has subsequently grown to become a global network of more than 40 chapters that mobilise against violence inflicted on Black communities by the state and vigilantes, and the hashtag has been much more widely adopted by many activists around the world, including those involved in mass protests against the police slaying of George Floyd.

Some critics of the movement view the slogan Black Lives Matter as a demand for preferential treatment, and attempt to counter it with the mantra "All Lives Matter". Yet the assertion that all lives are equally valuable in a liberal racial-capitalist world order is precisely what the BLM movement challenges, pointing to the many ways in which Black life has historically been, and continues to be, devalued, debased and destroyed.

Scholars who think critically about race locate the origins of contemporary disregard for Black life in the system of racial chattel slavery that developed over four centuries in the Atlantic World (for instance, Crenshaw et al., 1996; Davis, 2003; Hartman, 2007; Kendi, 2016). That system became the backbone of extremely lucrative global markets in sugar, coffee, tobacco, cotton, and other cash crops. These markets, and the economic activities that supported them, including shipping, insurance, and banking, allowed some individuals, groups, cities and nations to grow rich and prosper. But for other people, they spelt death.

Over the centuries during which Africans fell victim to the transatlantic slave trade, millions of women, men and children died en route to the Americas, and the life expectancy of those who survived the journey was, at many times and in many places, astonishingly brief. These innumerable deaths were not deliberately planned and orchestrated with a view to exterminating Africans. Instead, as Saidiya Hartman (2007: 31) observes, they were of the type that some today would describe as "collateral damage", incidental to the acquisition of profit and to the rise of capitalism. And, Hartman continues, incidental death "occurs when life has no normative value, when no humans are involved". The only value that attached to the lives of the mass of enslaved Africans was their monetary value as objects of exchange, the value that could be extracted from their bodily capacity to labour, and in some contexts, to reproduce the next generation of enslaved workers.

Central to the logic of Atlantic World slavery was an assumed line between those human beings whose lives mattered, and those whose lives did not. The latter were imagined as aliens, outsiders, enslave-able and expendable beings. Though they had a duty to labour for their legal owners and were criminally liable for any crime they committed, they did not merit the rights and protections afforded to those human beings who were socially recognised as full persons and members of the political community. The legal abolition of chattel slavery did not erase this line. Instead, the imagined division between "nobodies" and "people of value" continued to be made material by laws, policies and practices in the post-abolition world with regard to three key areas: land, labour, and mobility; citizenship and rights; and criminalisation and violence. Through them, forms of exclusion and inequality that were foundational to Atlantic World slavery continue to reach into the present moment.

Land, labour and mobility

One of the problems that the legal abolition of slavery in the nineteenth century presented political rulers of former slave societies and colonies was ostensibly economic. Until abolition, the backbreaking field labour of enslaved people was the lifeblood of plantation economies in the American South, the Caribbean, and Brazil. If slavery's legal abolition freed enslaved people and their descendants from such labour, it would constitute a profound threat to national, colonial, and global economies. What if, instead of becoming a source of wage labour for the plantations, emancipated people chose to eke out an independent subsistence off the land? And even if they accepted wage labour, what if, now free owners of their own labour power, they left the plantation regions and set off to areas, countries or cities where they could find better wages and working conditions, and/or mobilised collectively to improve conditions?

These threats to elite interests were addressed in a number of ways. In the British Caribbean, colonial officials supported slaveholders after the legal abolition of slavery in 1834 by introducing an apprenticeship system that legally bound "emancipated" people to their former owners until 1838, and more importantly, by paying them compensation for their loss of their human property on abolition. Indeed, in 1833, the British government took out one of the largest loans in history to compensate slave owners, borrowing £20 million – a sum that at the time represented around 5 per cent of British GDP and almost half of the government's annual expenditure, and is today equivalent to £308 billion (Craemer, 2021). It was only in 2015 that British taxpayers finished paying off this debt. The French and the Dutch also made compensation payments to slaveholders on abolition.

Those released from slavery did not receive a penny. Instead, they actually lost their customary rights of access to small plots of subsistence land. Under slavery, planters had saved themselves the expense and trouble of purchasing and distributing provisions by allowing the enslaved to grow food. After abolition, "provision plots" threatened to reduce emancipated people's dependence on wage labour, and planters moved to destroy them. Even fruit trees that grew wild in the vicinity of plantations were cut down with a view to ensuring that unless they accepted waged work, the "free" would starve.

At the same time, former plantation slaves lost their customary rights to shelter, now becoming "tenants" of their former owners. Wage/rent contracts were set in place, whereby tenancy was conditional on the performance of plantation labour. Breaches of such agreements by tenants were punishable with fines or imprisonment, or "ejectment" from their homes. In addition, legislation was passed to outlaw "squatting" public land, and impede the purchase of land by the formerly enslaved. The impact of such measures continued to shape patterns of land ownership in the twentieth century. Meanwhile, the mobility of the newly emancipated was constrained by vagrancy laws and emigration controls, designed to prevent "freed" people from escaping the misery and poverty of the wage/rent system by moving elsewhere.

In the US, compensation was also paid to some slave owners through an 1862 Act that provided $300 for each enslaved person released from bondage. The number freed in this way was around 3,100, at a cost to the state of over $930,000, the equivalent of around $25 million today (Craemer, 2021). As the Civil War drew towards an end in 1865, a Special Field Order did also proclaim that freed families should be granted plots of land and the means by which to farm it ("40 acres and a mule"). But that order was soon annulled. Land that had been allocated to the formerly enslaved was mostly returned to its pre-war white owners. Following abolition in December 1865, restrictions on "freed" people buying or even renting land were set in place.

Land ownership remained firmly concentrated in the hands of the white planter class, to whom formerly enslaved people now often came to be bound through a system known as "sharecropping". In exchange for a share of the crops they produced, landowners rented families small plots of land, and advanced them seeds, tools, clothing and food. But landowners were in a position to manipulate the arrangement to their own advantage, and once sharecroppers were indebted to the landowner, which they invariably became, they could not legally leave the landowner's property. In the US too, vagrancy laws formed another part of the armoury used to compel "freed" people to provide labour for landowners. To be on the move without proof of employment and a fixed abode was a crime.

Legal abolition came much later in Brazil, in 1888. By then, much of its vast population of enslaved people had already achieved free status by other means. Those who remained in slavery were largely concentrated in poorer agricultural regions of the country, often on sugar plantations that by the end of the nineteenth century were becoming increasingly unviable economically. As in the rest of the Americas, they received no compensation on emancipation, and found themselves formally free but landless. Again there were efforts to legally restrict land purchase, but regardless of such measures, the absence of alternative livelihood opportunities meant that many of the newly emancipated and their dependants continued to live and work in much the same conditions endured under slavery, often on the estates of their former owners. To this day, patterns of land ownership in Brazil express and reproduce vast inequalities – 10 per cent of the largest properties occupy 73 per cent of the country's agricultural land (Tradehub, 2019).

Denied compensation and land, and often concentrated in regions that were beginning to stagnate economically as a result of global economic developments, many formerly enslaved people and their descendants were willing to move for paid work. They came to constitute a pool of workers that employers could call on when facing labour shortages and/or to drive down wages (what Marxists might call a "reserve army of labour"). In the Caribbean from the mid-nineteenth through to the twentieth century, thousands migrated within the region as well as to Central and Latin America and the US, to meet demand for labour on infrastructure projects such as the construction of railroads and the Panama Canal, as well as in factories, mines, and banana, coffee and sugar plantations. In the post World War II period, British employers, especially British Rail, the NHS, and London Transport, addressed the dire shortage of labour they faced by recruiting workers from British colonies, including those in the Caribbean. In the US and Brazil too, many formerly enslaved people and their descendants were recruited to work in more industrially developed regions of their countries, sometimes specifically in order to break strikes, as well as to meet labour shortages.

Whether they remained in the areas where their forebears had been enslaved on plantations, or moved to industrially developed regions, the descendants of the formerly enslaved and colonised continued to be subject to forms of hyper-exploitation. Throughout the twentieth century, they were concentrated in the most difficult, dirty and dangerous work, for the lowest pay, and on the most precarious terms; paying the highest rents for

the poorest accommodation; with least access to social rights and protections. That pattern remains in place today. In fact, descendants of the
formerly enslaved and colonised are disproportionately present amongst
the informal sector and migrant workforces discussed earlier. Phenomena
described as "modern slavery" are bound up in the Afterlives of slavery
and colonialism. And the hyper-exploitability of these groups connects
to a second set of laws, policies and practices that were pursued in the
post-abolition world.

Race, rights and citizenship

Another challenge that abolition posed for those who governed former
slave societies was ostensibly political, and concerned whether and
how to incorporate the formerly enslaved population and their descendants into the political community as "free" people. Pro-slavery thinkers
had long justified the enslavement of Africans and their descendants by
using tropes of people racialised as Black as lazy, childlike, dependent,
untrustworthy, heathen, promiscuous, thieving, irrational beings. Though
they decried the cruelties of slavery, many white antislavery thinkers
(William Wilberforce provides one example) did not actually reject these
racist ideas, and often also believed enslaved Africans and their descendants were "primitive" people, unready for freedom in modern societies.
What if, emancipated from slavery, they demanded rights and liberties
equal to their white superiors? If they were free to publicly practise their
"primal" religions, and indulge in unchaste and dissolute behaviours?
What if they refused to accept their "proper" place in a social order strictly
hierarchised by class, gender and race?

The way in which political elites responded to these "problems" in the
United States is probably the most familiar story, as its post-abolition history of segregating and oppressing people imagined as having even "one
drop of Black blood" is well known. In the early nineteenth century, many
slave states of the US had quite sizeable populations of "free people of
colour" who did actually enjoy some of the rights enjoyed by free white
people, but this changed as the institution of slavery came under growing
threat. White elites' mounting anxiety about slave revolts and the prospect
of abolition encouraged state legislators to pass laws restricting freedoms
of free people of colour, and by the 1850s, the idea that those racialised
as Black or with Black ancestry carried a "taint of blood" that disqualified

them from citizenship in a white state was well established. Even Abraham Lincoln, celebrated as an abolitionist, believed it would be impossible to assimilate those with visible African ancestry into the existing social order as free people. Like many other white abolitionists, he therefore initially favoured a policy of deportation, whereby emancipated people would be transported to colonies in Africa, such as Liberia, or to Haiti or Panama.

One frequently overlooked element of US history is the fact that enslaved people themselves played a central role in the Civil War, participating in a General Strike to weaken the Confederate economy, escaping across enemy lines, fighting for the Unionist army. For a short period after the war's end in 1865, they also successfully struggled for inclusion in the political processes by which the meaning of freedom would be established. In 1870, the 15th Amendment to the Constitution ruled that states could not deny the right to vote on grounds of "race, color, or previous condition of servitude". Some people racialised as Black were elected to public office. In 1875, the Civil Rights Act asserted the "equality of all men before the law", and prohibited discrimination on the basis of colour, race or previous condition of servitude in public places and facilities.

The backlash came quickly, however. In 1883, the Supreme Court declared the Civil Rights Act unconstitutional, paving the way for the passage of Jim Crow laws that codified previously private and informal racist practices, mandating the racial segregation of schools, hospitals, public transport, public space, restrooms, hotels, restaurants, theatres, and even drinking fountains. This body of law re-established the dishonoured, alien and subordinate condition that had been imposed on enslaved African people and their descendants by slave status. It remained in place until the Civil Rights Act of 1964 and the Voting Rights Act of 1965. In the words of sociologist W. B. Du Bois, "The slave went free; stood for a brief moment in the sun; then moved back again toward slavery" (1935: 30).

British Caribbean colonies

Ensuring that the formerly enslaved remained "in their place" post-abolition was a different, and in some senses easier task for the British, since after brief efforts at constitutional change, Britain had taken most of its Caribbean colonies back into Crown Colony government by 1866. This was a form of government deemed necessary by British colonial officials because "the large numbers of an inferior race, and the baneful effects of slavery" made representative institutions and self-government impossible until such time as those of African descent could be "civilised". When Crown Colony rule was later modified to allow limited self-rule, voting rights remained conditional on property ownership. Universal adult suffrage was only attained in Jamaica in 1944 and in other colonies not until 1962. The formerly enslaved were thus mostly disbarred from participating in the political processes by which the meaning of freedom was established, and social hierarchies preserved.

However, because they were born on territories under British Colonial rule, descendants of enslaved people were citizens of the UK and Colonies. Under the British Nationality Act of 1948, all such citizens (known as Commonwealth Citizens) were entitled to live and work in the UK. People from Jamaica, Trinidad and Tobago and other islands under British colonial rule who arrived in post-war Britain on ships such as the *Empire Windrush* to assist the "motherland" in her hour of need faced no immigration controls on entry. They did, however, face profound racism, an exclusionary and often violent force that permeated all aspects of daily life, and from which the law did not even formally offer any protection until the 1965 Race Relations Act. As with Civil Rights legislation in the US, this did not undo centuries of prejudice (and did not even outlaw racial discrimination in all areas of public life). Commonwealth citizens from the Caribbean, also Africa and South Asia, continued to be stigmatised and excluded from the rights and recognitions enjoyed by white citizens.

Moreover, when Black and brown Commonwealth Citizens acted on the formal equality the law granted them by actually moving to live in the white motherland, it triggered such a powerful racist backlash amongst white Britons that the UK government moved to restrict their mobility. The Commonwealth Immigrants Act of 1962 was introduced to end the free movement of Commonwealth Citizens, who now became subject to immigration controls. In 1971, a system of immigration control was introduced that in theory regulated the entry and stay of people of all nationalities without right of abode in the UK, but in practice focused heavily on restricting the entry of people from countries where a majority of the population is racialised as Black or brown.

That system was further tightened by successive Labour and Conservative governments, and the "hostile environment" policy was introduced by the Conservative-Liberal Democrat coalition Government in 2012. As described earlier, this entailed a set of administrative and legislative measures deliberately designed to make daily life unbearable for people without leave to remain in the country. To access public and private services necessary to sustain life (housing, bank accounts, work, health care) it was now necessary to produce evidence of the right to be present in the UK. Using the decades old language of racist graffiti, the Home Office ran an advertising campaign that warned "illegal immigrants" to "GO HOME OR FACE ARREST".

Yet many of those who had entered perfectly legally as children of Commonwealth Citizens in the 1940s, 50s and 60s, who had been schooled, worked and paid taxes for their entire adult lives in the UK, could not produce documents to demonstrate their right of abode, since no such documents had ever been issued to them. This led to what became known as the Windrush Scandal, whereby people suffering cancer and other life threatening diseases were refused hospital treatment, others lost their jobs, or were forcibly detained and deported to their country of birth, even though they often had not set foot there since early childhood. These events very clearly demonstrated the precarious and second class nature of the rights and freedoms held by Britons racialised as Black or brown.

Brazil

On first inspection, questions about race and rights look different in post-abolition Brazil. Here, while Blackness, and more particularly Africanness, was stigmatised, colonialism had generated systems of racial classification that produced extensively graded colour hierarchies. Differences in wealth and political standing reflected, but did not perfectly map onto, a hierarchy based on skin tone and ancestry. Long before abolition in 1888, free and propertied men even of the darkest skin tone were deemed fit for citizenship by the Brazilian Constitution of 1824, providing they were born in Brazil, not Africa. At the same time, however, a series of other restrictions on political rights (such as income and literacy requirements for suffrage) operated to ensure that few Brazilians racialised as Black would enjoy formal political rights, even after emancipation (Chalhoub, 2006).

Following abolition, there was no equivalent of Jim Crow apartheid in Brazil, in fact, the nation came to be mythologised as a "racial democracy". Nonetheless, the valorisation of whiteness, encouraged in the latter half of the nineteenth century by the circulation of European racist evolutionary theories, had informed a widespread notion that the genetic quality of the country's population could be improved by a process of *branquea-mento*, or "whitening". With this in mind, the 1891 constitution prohibited African and Asian immigration into the country while the immigration of white Europeans was actively encouraged, including by subsidising their steamship passage.

Moreover, despite being formally ascribed rights of citizenship, Afro-Brazilians continued to face racism in labour and housing markets, and other areas of social life. Today, they remain overrepresented in difficult, poorly paid, dangerous and precarious work, in poorer peripheral dwellings without access to water and sanitation, and underrepresented in higher education, and political and public life. They also remain at disproportionate risk of violence, in ways and for reasons that highlight commonalities between Brazil, the US, and the British Caribbean in terms of their post-abolition histories.

Criminalisation and violence

Violence or its threat was an integral feature of enslaved people's daily lives. Many owners and/or their representatives used violence as a means of exacting labour and submission to their rule, and rape of enslaved women and girls by masters and others under their employ was commonplace. Even if their owners eschewed such brutalities, as some did, the enslaved remained at risk of violence from both state and private actors if they acted, or were perceived to have acted, in ways that challenged the laws and social mores of slave society. The passage of acts of abolition did nothing to address the systems of surveillance, criminalisation, punishment and arbitrary violence that had worked to keep the enslaved in their social place. Those systems were instead adjusted and honed to keep the formerly enslaved and their descendants fixed in their newly allotted place as lowly, hyper-exploitable wage labourers.

Policing and violence in the British Caribbean

In Jamaica, the abolition of slavery in 1834 was accompanied by the passage of a Police Act, which established a militarised police force that would, in effect, perform the function previously undertaken by slave patrols. Colonial police officers and Black "constables" enforced the vagrancy laws that criminalised strategies used by the poor to survive.

Prostitution and other "disreputable" forms of behaviour (including sodomy which was criminalised by British colonial law) were a particular focus of violent law enforcement. Flogging was removed from the penal system on the abolition of slavery, but then reintroduced as a possible punishment for male convicts in 1850. When the formerly enslaved and their descendants sought to collectively express political grievances, the authorities responded with brute, often lethal, force.

By the early twentieth century, colonial police forces in the British Caribbean were increasingly preoccupied by the political threats to the status quo. In the 1930s, the region experienced a wave of mass strikes and anti-colonial protests against low wages, high unemployment, racist colonial officials, and lack of structures for representation or collective bargaining. The police responded by harassing and intimidating labour leaders, beating protestors with clubs and batons, and in some cases, shooting and killing them. As was the case under slavery, the primary function of policing was not to protect the working people, but to preserve a hierarchical social order and secure the interests of the state and elites. As in other post-abolition societies, this function was fulfilled by private actors as well as state security forces.

In Jamaica, plantation owners and private companies hired armed vigilantes to control labour and assist state forces with the political surveillance and suppression of the "lower orders" (Jaffe and Diphoorn, 2019). Moreover, while still under colonial rule, political parties built patron-client relationships with particular communities, generating conflicts or "turf wars". The latter became increasingly bloody following an influx of firearms in the 1970s, including those shipped to Jamaica by the CIA to arm opponents of Michael Manley, whose brand of democratic socialism was regarded as a threat to US interests in the region. In the months leading up to the 1980 election, an estimated 800 people were killed.

Guns have continued to flow into Jamaica, ever since, mostly from the US, and the country has acquired a reputation for violent crime. There are areas of the island that still have some of the highest homicide rates in the world, and murders are often associated with drugs trading and other criminal activities. But unlawful killing is not merely a problem associated with area "dons", narcotics traffickers and other criminals. Between 2000 and 2016, members of the Jamaican Constabulary Force are estimated to have killed some 3,000 people from poor and marginalised communities, including extrajudicial executions on the orders of some governmental authorities (Amnesty International, 2016b). Meanwhile, across the Caribbean, the private security industry has grown rapidly since the 1990s. In some countries, there are as many or more private security employees than police officers. Private security guards employed to protect businesses, tourism enclaves and gated housing estates are typically poorly paid and work long hours, and are generally expected to carry small arms or light weapons. Cases of them being attacked and even killed during robberies are not uncommon; neither are reports of them using arbitrary violence against individuals they perceive as "up to no good".

Policing and violence in Brazil

In Brazil, a militarised police force was first established in Rio de Janeiro in the early nineteenth century, when the Portuguese royal family took its Court of some 15,000 people there. Enslaved people made up more than half the city's population, and in the wake of the Haitian revolution, elite groups' anxieties about slave revolt were running high. The role of the Military Division of the Royal Police Guard formed in 1809 was to prevent this and ensure public order, and its activities focused almost exclusively on the enslaved and free people racialised as Black and *pardo* (mixed and/or indigenous), who were frequent victims of random beatings and public whippings. Expressions of what were deemed to be African culture, especially practising the martial art of *capoeira*, or spiritual practices associated with *candomblé*, were viciously repressed. More generally, the police violently suppressed customs and practices of the poor as well as the enslaved, in particular their use of public space for recreation, unsanctioned economic activities, and any behaviour deemed dirty, immoral, or uncivil (drinking, gambling, begging, prostitution, swearing, making insulting gestures, and so on).

The abolition of slavery did nothing to alter this. Without access to land and facing racist discrimination in labour markets, the formerly enslaved joined the ranks of the "free" poor. They thus continued to form part of class perceived as dangerous and criminal and therefore subject to the arbitrary violence of a military-style police, as well as from vigilante groups. Such violence continues to pose a threat to Brazil's poor and marginalised communities today. In the past decade, police have killed 33,000 people, 9,000 in Rio de Janeiro alone. Of the latter, more than 75 per cent of those murdered were Black men. In 2019, 75 per cent of people killed by the military Police in all Brazil were Afro-Brazilian (*preto* and *pardo*), a group that represents 56 per cent of the population. Human Rights Watch has documented the fact that in poor neighbourhoods, police open fire routinely and recklessly, killing child and adult bystanders as well as those they are targeting. As in Jamaica, Brazilian police are known to be involved in extrajudicial executions (Muñoz, 2020). Vigilante violence, including grotesquely brutal lynching, is also an ever present threat to dwellers in poor neighbourhoods, especially those racialised as Black and those who step outside conservative norms of gender and sexuality, such as gay men and trans women. Some estimates suggest that one person is lynched daily in Brazil today (Swift, 2018).

Policing and violence in the United States

The same basic story is repeated in the US, where after abolition, slave patrols and night watches became the armed police units that violently enforced vagrancy and Jim Crow legislation. Here too, private actors also continued to perpetrate sickening violence against the formerly enslaved. Landowners employed armed security to oversee sharecroppers. White citizens mobilised as attack mobs and vigilante groups (such as the Ku Klux Klan, formed in the 1860s) that brutalised and lynched "free" Black people who attempted to assert, or were perceived as asserting, their rights to freedom or equality. It is estimated that in Southern States alone, more than 4,000 African Americans, including children, were lynched by white mobs between 1877 and 1950.

The violence and poverty faced by those racialised as Black in the South prompted what is known as "The Great Migration". Between 1915 and 1970, some 6 million African-Americans journeyed from Southern States to seek refuge in cities of the Northeast, Midwest and West of the US. They did not escape white racism in so doing. Cities in the north, including Chicago, witnessed white mobs looting, burning, beating and killing in districts where Black people from the south had settled. And throughout the first half of the twentieth century, racism in the labour and real estate markets, as well as in state housing, employment and education policies, led to increasing residential segregation along racial lines in Northern cities, and the emergence of "ghettoes". The pockets of deprivation and poverty into which Black people had been forced by violent and exclusionary racism were then interpreted as threatening dens of criminality, and "proof" that African Americans were racially inferior and still unready for freedom. These districts became the focus of intense and violent policing, policing that has been further militarised in recent decades. A recent study (GBD, 2021) estimates that 30,800 people died at the hands of the police in the US between 1980 and 2018, and found that the mortality rate due to police violence was 0.69 per 100,000 people racialised as Black, compared with 0.2 for people racialised as white.

Slavery and prisons

Slavery was never completely legally abolished in the US. The 13th Amendment to the US Constitution outlawed slavery except "as punishment for crime". Thus, in the post-abolition era, formerly enslaved people and their descendants could, when convicted of petty offences such as vagrancy, be lawfully re-enslaved. In 1880, the state of Louisiana purchased an 8000-acre plantation named Angola, which it converted into a prison. Slave quarters became cells to house formerly enslaved inmates, who were then forced to work the plantation as enslaved people had before them, but under the lash of the prison guard instead of the slave driver and for the profit of the state, rather than a private slaveholder. Today, Angola is the largest maximum security prison in the US, and its prisoners – of whom around 78 per cent are racialised as Black – still work the now 18,000 acre plantation, under conditions virtually identical to those endured by their enslaved forebears (Childs, 2015).

The caveat in the 13th Amendment also made it possible to develop a convict lease system whereby prisoners could be contracted out as forced labour to private enterprises. As a result, in the late nineteenth and early twentieth centuries, thousands of African Americans continued to be subject to brutally violent regimes of coerced and unpaid labour in lumber camps, brickyards, railroads, farms, plantations and other privately owned businesses. There is evidence that arrest rates correlated with demand for cheap labour. Death rates among convicts leased to private companies was extraordinarily high, and the vast majority of those exploited and killed in this way were Black. The convict lease system ended at different times in different states in the twentieth century. Prisoners in the US still work, but generally for the highly profitable Federal government-owned corporation UNICOR or other state-level prison industries, rather than for private businesses. Yet they still often work under threat of punishment, and the compulsion to do so is intensified in many states by the imposition of "room and board" fees that charge inmates for their own incarceration. The US has the highest incarceration rate in the world, and the largest number of prisoners – over 2 million in 2020. Mass incarceration was triggered by the "War on Drugs" that started under Nixon and gathered steam in the 1980s under the Regan administration, with its more general determination to be seen as "tough on crime". This fuelled a vast project of prison construction in which private corporations were heavily involved. Gross racial disparities in the criminal justice system mean that around two-thirds of prisoners in the US are people of colour. If released, most prisoners re-enter society deeply in debt, to face legally authorised discrimination in employment, housing, education, and public benefits. Criminalisation also leads to the temporary or permanent loss of formal political rights. An estimated 2.2 million Americans are disenfranchised by state laws that restrict voting rights even to those on probation or parole, and after a sentence is spent. African Americans are disproportionately affected, with 1.8 million Black citizens banned from voting (Chung, 2021).

Prison expansion has also been a feature of Brazilian and British experience since the 1990s. Brazil's prison population is currently the third largest in the world, behind only China and the U.S. More than 755,000 people were incarcerated in 2019, and its prison population is projected to reach 1.5 million by 2025. In the UK, where the prison population rose by 69 per cent between 1988 and 2018, there is actually greater disproportionality in the number of Black people in prisons than in the United States. People from ethnic minority backgrounds form only about 14 per cent of the general population in England and Wales, but make up around 27 per cent of the prison population, and if we narrow down to those who are racialised as Black, the statistics look worse still. They make up 3.3 per cent of the general population but 13 per cent of the prison population (Prison Reform Trust, 2019).

The price paid by those who are imprisoned for any offence, including minor drug offenses, has also risen exponentially for people who were born outside the UK, such as the children of Commonwealth migrants. The passage of the 2014 Immigration Act has facilitated the rapid expulsion of "Foreign National Prisoners" (FNPs) on release from prison. An "FNP" may have been brought to the UK as a baby or child, and/or may have a partner and children and all their friendship and kinship networks in the UK. Over 80 per cent of FNPs are imprisoned for non-violent offences. But where UK-born national prisoners can return to and move on with their lives after their sentence is spent, those who happen to have been born abroad are torn from all they know and love and permanently exiled to an unfamiliar and often hostile place. Again, this is a policy that disproportionately affects people racialised as Black or brown (De Noronha, 2020).

The future created by slavery

Acts of abolition delegitimised the treatment of human being as objects of property exchange and ownership. They did not completely erase the many laws, customs and practices designed to designate Africans and their descendants as a permanently dishonoured and subordinate subclass of human being, or compensate them for the violations and exploitation to which they had been subjected. Though operated in a world without legal chattel slavery, the structures, systems and practices described above continued to produce a subclass of people who, precisely because they were socially devalued and expendable, could be exploited more intensively and comprehensively than other workers. Throughout the twentieth century, anticolonial, civil rights, and antiracist activists fought to transform these structures, systems and practices, and their achievements are many and remarkable. Yet inequalities rooted in the history of Atlantic World slavery and the architecture of its abolition continue to differentially shape lives and the value that is attached to them in the twenty-first century.

The reach of slavery's past into the present of policing and criminal justice systems has already been described, but these inequalities affect all aspects of Black life, right from the start. In the US, Brazil and the UK, infant deaths per 1000 live births amongst the Black population are almost twice the national average. In the US, only 28 per cent of people racialised as Black graduated from college in 2016, compared to 42 per cent of those racialised as white. The poverty rate amongst Black Americans is almost triple that amongst those racialised as white; home ownership rates are significantly lower, and the median household income for Black Americans is around $20,000 less than that for white Americans. The unemployment rate amongst Black Americans has remained about twice that of white Americans for the past 50 years. There are also huge and persistent racial disparities in terms of health (Pollock, 2021). In the Covid-19 pandemic, the death rate amongst Black Americans has been almost 2.5 times higher than that of white Americans.

The US is frequently imagined as uniquely appalling in terms of racial inequality, but in the UK, Black people are ten times more likely than white to be stopped and searched by the police, police figures show that Black people were up to eight times more likely to be tasered by police than white people in 2018–19, and Black and Asian people were disproportionately fined for non-compliance with Covid-19 lockdown arrangements in 2020 (Amnesty International, 2021). White Britons are almost twice as likely to own their own homes than are people racialised as Black, and the unemployment rate of Black Britons was almost twice that of white Britons between 2004 and 2018. There are also significant racial disparities with regard to health, and Covid-19 deaths have also been disproportionately concentrated amongst Black and ethnic minority populations in the UK. In the Caribbean, meanwhile, as well as being plagued by the forms of violence, exclusion and labour exploitation outlined above, the health and wellbeing of most of the Black population is negatively impacted by the neoliberal economic reforms, SAPs and austerity measures that were discussed earlier.

what should we do about slavery?

The injustices and violence highlighted by "modern slavery" campaigners are inextricably bound up with the histories of slavery and colonialism, of concern to "Afterlives of slavery" thinkers. Yet, as will be seen, the two perspectives generate very different answers to the question of what we should do about slavery. Working on the assumption that "modern slavery" is a phenomenon antithetical to the values and norms of the existing liberal world order, antislavery NGOs forge a variety of alliances with governmental and supranational governmental organisations, businesses, religious organisations, media groups, smaller NGOs, and members of the public, to pursue a range of actions to combat the problem. The limitations of their main recommendations are considered below.

Tackling "modern slavery" in supply chains

Antislavery NGOs encourage businesses to combat "modern slavery" by committing to "Corporate Social Responsibility" (CSR) initiatives to root the problem out of their supply chains, and call on consumers to add pressure to this demand by boycotting companies that fail to do so. Because "modern slavery" is cast as a peculiarly repugnant form of criminality, it is imagined as external to and separate from ordinary, lawful business practices and the structures of the economic and political systems that underpin and are reproduced by the activities of "good" firms. This means that businesses, including corporate giants such as Coca-Cola, ExxonMobil, Ford, Microsoft and ManpowerGroup, are happy to jump aboard the "anti-trafficking and modern slavery" bandwagon. Indeed, though examples of the labour abuses that are produced by the mainstream supply chain business model have been continuously uncovered since the 1990s, large corporations have managed to reposition themselves as part of the solution to, rather than the cause of, labour abuse through their willingness to engage with antislavery initiatives (Le Baron, 2020).

The type of actions identified as CSR best practice by antislavery NGOs include efforts to improve labour policies, monitor suppliers to ensure they meet labour standards, participate in fair trade, and engage in charitable giving. There is nothing wrong with such advice, and it is clearly better if corporations make such efforts than if they don't. But are they enough to ring in any real change? "Modern slavery" in supply chains has now been constructed as a risk to corporate reputations, and corporations often behave in the same way with this risk as with any other. Responsibility for monitoring supply chains is passed down the line to smaller suppliers, who are required to hire auditors and return reports to the TNC, or secure ethical certification from one of a number of schemes that will then allow the TNC to report that it has taken steps to ensure the ethicality of its suppliers. But it does not follow that TNCs are willing to pay enough for certificated products to ensure that it is viable for their suppliers to stop squeezing labour costs. For this reason, research reported by LeBaron (2020) suggests that labour conditions are much the same for workers producing both certified and uncertified tea and cocoa, for example.

Moreover, CSR activities are largely voluntary. Though some governments have introduced legislation that demands compliance with certain measures, such legislation does not criminalise corporate failure to eliminate labour abuse from supply chains, and often merely requires businesses to conduct audits and report on their efforts to avoid profiting from forms of labour exploitation dubbed "modern slavery". The UK's Modern Slavery Act (2015) is a case in point. At the same time as politely asking businesses to take greater responsibility for monitoring and controlling their supply chains, governments around the world have increasingly stepped back from labour law enforcement.

Recent research found that across the EU, safety inspections have been cut by a fifth since 2010, and 1000 fewer labour inspectors are now available to visit workplaces. The ILO states that, at a minimum, there should be one labour inspector per 10,000 workers. Today, over one third of European countries do not meet that standard (ETUC, 2021). In the UK, there is now just one labour market inspector per 20,000 workers, and cuts to HMRC's national minimum wage inspectors mean that statistically, employers can expect to receive a visit once every 500 years (Unchecked, 2020). In the US, the federal work safety watchdog Occupational Safety and Health Administration, had cut workplace safety inspectors to the lowest level in its 48-year history by 2019, to just one compliance officer for every 59,000 workers. The absence of labour inspection disproportionately impacts migrant workers, one of the groups known to be overrepresented amongst workplace deaths.

Given the above, antislavery NGOs' calls for consumer action are also unlikely to prove transformative. Yes, it is preferable to avoid buying from companies that have been exposed as responsible for labour abuses if you are in a position to do so. But the emphasis on consumers' power to lead change through their individual moral actions ignores the massive differences amongst consumers in terms of wealth and privilege. Single parents in low waged employment in the UK or the US may be well aware that cheap garments or canned foods have likely been produced by other exploited workers, for example, but lack the spending power to choose fair trade or "slave free" alternatives. The luxury of "ethical consumption" is even less accessible to the vast majority of ordinary people in global south countries. Certainly, there are many reasons why privileged consumers can and should consume less and pay more for what they consume, and campaigns to raise awareness of, and challenge, the labour abuse from which TNCs' profit are politically important. But consumer-led boycotts of non-certified goods are not an effective substitute for the kind of measures known historically to have made wage-labour look less like slavery for privileged groups of global north workers – which is to say, unionisation, laws to constrain employers, and labour inspections, coupled with adequate provision of welfare and social protection.

Antislavery NGOs' simplistic messages about each individual's power to "gift freedom" through their practices of consumption, like their calls on corporations to adopt CSR measures, deflect attention from the complex and challenging political work that needs to be done to transform the global financial and trade structures and institutions that today underpin and reproduce inequality and extreme labour exploitation. At a minimum, there should be greater engagement with sector-based worker-driven initiatives that seek to redistribute value from the top to the bottom of the supply chain as well as worker-driven social responsibility measures in general; more rather than less labour inspections and stronger enforcement of existing labour laws; legal change to establish joint liability between corporations at the head of supply chains and their suppliers (LeBaron, 2020). But even if corporations' capacity to pass risk and costs down supply chains was much more effectively constrained, it would not force them to desist from all practices known to create vulnerability to precarious labour, such as buying vast tracts of subsistence land and turning it over to the production of cash crops.

Moreover, recent research shows that rich countries of the global north continue to drain global south countries of trillions of dollars through processes of unequal exchange. Because wages paid to workers in the south are on average one-fifth the level of northern wages, every unit imported by the south must be paid for by the export of many more units to the north. In this way, the global north appropriates tens of billions of tonnes of raw materials and hundreds of billions of hours of human labour each year, labour that is embodied both in primary commodities, and in the high-tech industrial goods that are now often manufactured in the South. The scale of unequal exchange increased significantly during the structural adjustment period of the 1980s and 1990s and remains a significant feature of the world economy. Rich countries continue to rely on imperial forms of appropriation to sustain their high levels of income and consumption – global north economies annually appropriate from the south commodities worth $2.2 trillion in northern prices, enough to end extreme poverty 15 times over (Hickel et al., 2021). While this continues, even global south governments that were wholeheartedly committed to guaranteeing labour rights and social protection to all on their territory would lack the economic wherewithal to do so.

"Raid and rescue"

As noted at the outset of the book, the contemporary antislavery movement includes both NGOs that can be characterised as secular, humanist and liberal in outlook, and NGOs that are much more socially conservative. Differences between the two are especially pronounced in relation to the sex sector. The former do not necessarily conflate prostitution and slavery.

In fact, in 1997, Antislavery International published an important report that called for prostitution to be redefined as sex work, and for full human and labour rights to be extended to sex workers. But socially conservative (and also radical feminist) NGOs often assume that sex commerce relies almost exclusively on naïve and vulnerable women and girls who have been tricked or lured into the trade by criminals, or who have made "poor" choices. Indeed, evangelical Christian antislavery NGOs more generally tend to work on the assumption that women and children, and members of poor communities in global south countries, stand in need of protection from themselves and their own choices and "traditions", as well as from others. They are therefore particularly prone to pressing for radical and invasive interventions known as "raid and rescue" to "redeem" victims.

The "raid and rescue" approach has been widely applied in global south countries, where large and well-funded global north antislavery NGOs such as Justice & Care and the International Justice Mission work with local police to conduct raids on brothels and other sites of informal labour to free slaves and support the prosecution of perpetrators. But since most sex workers have chosen, or choose to remain in, this form of work, these missions are unwelcome to many of those they purport to help. For example, in a recent study almost 80 per cent of women removed from sex work in India through such "rescues" stated that they had been working of their own volition and had been 'rescued' against their wills (Walters, 2019). The "raid and rescue" approach also disregards the extensive evidence on police brutality against sex workers and simply positions law enforcers as the "good guys". "Wherever we work", explains Justice & Care (2018), "we do so alongside the state. We do all we can to strengthen the role of the state". But as states are very often patriarchal, and the stigma against female prostitution is strong, in addition to the violence of raids themselves, rescue missions often lead to one form of captivity being replaced by another.

In India, for instance, women and girls "liberated" in raids are typically transferred to prisons or locked shelters or "protection homes" where they can be confined for months or years. There have been numerous scandals involving rape, beatings, forced labour, suicide and self-harm in such settings. If returned to their original villages, the stigma that attaches to sex workers is such that they are socially, sometimes violently, excluded. Meanwhile, as elsewhere in the world, those who end up being prosecuted for trafficking offences are not the powerful, evil villains of antislavery folklore, but mostly drawn from the same marginalised and impoverished population as sex workers themselves. Indeed, often, they are former sex workers who have progressed to becoming brothel managers or recruitment agents. A study of people imprisoned for trafficking offences in Cambodia, for instance, found that of 427 people incarcerated for human trafficking in six prisons between 1997 and 2007, 80 per cent were female, poor, with very limited education, and had large families with five to eight children (Keo, 2013: 84).

The "raid and rescue" approach leads to equally problematic outcomes when applied in sectors other than sex work. Academic research on US-based Evangelical Christian NGOs' partnerships with Ghanaian police officers to "rescue" children involved in fishing on Lake Volta in Ghana, for example, suggests such raids have indiscriminately and often violently removed children who were actually with their own families. Members of local communities affected regard these "rescues" as kidnaps, but lack the financial and social power it would require to hold the NGOs and police accountable for the wrongful abduction of their children, or to contest the framing of their children as slaves and recover them from the rehabilitation centres where they are held (Okyere et al., 2021).

Indeed, it is notable that the "raiding" approach is only consistently applied in settings where those affected are impoverished, socially marginalised, stigmatised and/or criminalised, such as fishing communities in Ghana, brothels and red light districts and other informal work sites around the world, traveller camps in the UK, and so on. The multi-million pound London homes of wealthy individuals are not raided by NGOs to check whether or not their domestic workers are being held in "modern slavery", even though it is known that some domestic workers are violently abused in such settings.

"Spotting the signs"

Similar problems arise with campaigns that urge members of the general public to report to the authorities concerns about "modern slavery" in global north worksites such as hand car washes, nail bars, cafes and restaurants. Some antislavery NGOs have developed "spot the signs" trainings and apps to encourage reporting. The "signs" we are told to look out for include workers whose body language appears fearful or withdrawn, who avoid eye contact, who are wearing unsuitable clothing for the work in hand, and who ask for payment in cash rather than accepting cards. But for reasons discussed earlier, informal sector workplaces are sites of livelihood opportunities as well as potential sites of abuse for those who are excluded from legal means of survival. All of the "signs" we are told to watch out for are as likely to indicate that someone is working without state sanction as they are to suggest that they are victims of "modern slavery".

By reporting their suspicions, members of the public do not only, or even necessarily, alert the authorities to the existence of severe exploitation, but also to the locations where asylum seekers and undocumented migrants are working illegally. In the UK, such reports are very helpful to Immigration Compliance and Enforcement (ICE) teams, given that, in theory at least, they are only supposed to question individuals who have come to their attention through "prior intelligence". Again, raids do not usually lead to "freedom". Even victims of violence and exploitation are likely to end up imprisoned or in detention. "Spot the Signs" trainings eagerly "educate" the public about so-called "modern slavery", but fail to educate them about the hostile environment deliberately created by the asylum and immigration regime, or warn them of the likely consequences of alerting the authorities to sites where asylum seekers and undocumented migrants work.

In fact, far from urging caution, such trainings counsel members of the public to act on their gut feelings. "By simply trusting your instinct and reporting your suspicions, you could spark a series of events leading to the rescue of many victims", one Local Authority information sheet on "human trafficking" tells us (Betterlivesleeds, 2016). In addition to the problems already mentioned, this advice gives people permission to act on their prejudices. Passengers on planes, flight attendants, hotel receptionists and others groups of front-line workers who have been given "spot the signs" training with regard to trafficking are emboldened to question and challenge the mobility of people and groups about whom they have a bad "gut feeling". This frequently translates into straight white Americans and Europeans feeling there must be "something wrong" if they see a Black woman travelling with a white man, or Black children travelling with white adults, or children travelling with two adults of the same gender. Because interracial couples and families, and gay families, are illegible to them as partners or families, they "spot the signs" of "trafficking and modern slavery", and there have been numerous reports of couples and parents being hauled aside and interrogated by police or immigration officials as a result of well-meaning interventions.

Some advocates of "spotting signs" are unapologetic about this unin-
tended consequence. It is better to be safe than sorry, they say, and inno-
cent people subject to harassment surely cannot object when they have
been inconvenienced in the noble cause of rescuing victims of "trafficking and modern slavery". I suspect they would not be so sanguine if *they*
were the ones who could not move without being routinely singled out
for intrusive and intimidating police and border agency interrogation. This
aside, the easy and repeated slippage between anti-trafficking and "modern slavery" measures and efforts to control the mobility of groups of people deemed somehow suspect, or lacking the capacity for freedom, ought
to trouble anyone genuinely concerned to promote and protect universal
human rights. It not only provides liberal states with a convenient justifi-
cation for policies that violate the rights of people on the move, but also
equips patriarchal governments with an excuse for gender discriminatory
policies. A number of countries, including Sri Lanka and Ethiopia in 2013,
Indonesia in 2015, and the Philippines in 2020, have banned or restricted
the overseas migration of certain categories of "low-skilled" women in
order to "protect" them from traffickers. Nepal and Kyrgyzstan are consid-
ering similar legislation.

Antislavery and immigration regimes

Because policies of inclusion and exclusion on grounds of immigration
regulations are known to create a range of vulnerabilities, a number of
international institutions and treaties have been established to articulate
and defend the rights of migrants. Though no single entity is mandated
or financed to protect migrants' rights across the board, their rights are
addressed to varying degrees and in different ways by the United Nations
Common System (UN), the International Labour Organisation (ILO), the
United Nations High Commissioner for Refugees (UNHCR), the UN Department for Social and Economic Affairs (DESA), the Global Migration Group
(GMG), the Office of the United Nations High Commissioner for Human
Rights (OHCHR) and a collection of special advisors and rapporteurs. The
International Organisation for Migration (IOM) is another key player in the
field of migration.

A number of antislavery NGOs align themselves with and support the
efforts of these international agencies. Walk Free, for example, recently
partnered with IOM to produce a report on migrants and their vulnerability

to trafficking, "modern slavery" and forced labour (IOM, 2019). Among other things, that report calls for measures to: protect those fleeing repressive regimes; address the threat of deportation and detention for migrants seeking redress from employment abuses; create ethical and safe, fee-free recruitment across borders; promote labour rights, inspections and protections; reduce discrimination. As with guidance on CSR, these recommendations are laudable, but can at best only partially ameliorate the problems they are intended to address.

The international entities that antislavery NGOs partner with are concerned to promote "orderly and safe migration", not freedom of movement. For instance, though it describes itself as an organisation *for* migration, a huge amount of the IOM's work is *against* migration. It disseminates knowledge of policies and technologies that most effectively control borders, assists in the construction of detention camps, operates schemes to return unwanted migrants, including to war torn countries, and runs "information seminars" designed to discourage migration. Its core objective is to manage migration. This is consonant with high-income states' ambitions to control the number and "type" of people who enter, but does not address the situation of large numbers of people on the move today.

Managing the orderly and safe passage of migrants whose movement is authorised by governments in order to fill gaps in labour markets, and protecting them from the worst excesses of exploitative recruiters and employers, may ameliorate the situation for some migrant workers. It leaves those who are "illegally" present on the territory unprotected, however. Again, antislavery NGOs are not blind to this, and do press states to mitigate the effects of criminalising migrants. But they do so very selectively. They have been part of successful campaigns for "victims of trafficking" and "modern slaves" to be added to the list of those who deserve to be afforded special protections under international human rights law, and have been amongst those who challenge states when they fail to provide such protections, as they frequently do.

Yet antislavery NGOs do not vigorously denounce *all* violence against *all* migrants perpetrated by liberal states. For example, in the UK, a number of antislavery NGOs joined with refugee and human rights NGOs to condemn the fact that "potential victims of trafficking" are routinely held in prison-like detention centres due to their immigration status, often for long periods (more than 1,200 were detained in 2019 alone). They called on the government to introduce an absolute bar on the detention of confirmed and potential victims of slavery, but stopped short of demanding an end to immigration detention *per se*. Likewise, when they speak of reducing discrimination against migrants, they do not mean the forms of discrimination licensed and mandated by states, such as the UK government's demand that landlords, employers, and health service providers discriminate against those who cannot produce papers demonstrating their right to rent, work, and access treatment. Indeed, it is this blind spot that leads them to disregard the potentially harmful consequences of the "sign spotting" interventions discussed above.

In the current viciously anti-migrant climate, and at a time when states are increasingly reneging on their commitments to human rights, it is good that some antislavery NGOs add their weight to calls to ensure vulnerable groups enjoy the protections to which they are entitled under international humanitarian law. But such calls do not and cannot address the abuses that spring from states' assertion of a right to control who is and is not admitted onto their territory and on what terms, nor can they address much of the violence that states use to enforce that claim. So long as it is deemed acceptable for states to treat some human beings as different from and lesser than others in terms of their rights and freedoms, there will be groups of people who are made vulnerable to forms of exploitation, abuse and violence by both state and non-state actors by the fact that their very presence on the territory is deemed "illegal".

What should we do about the Afterlives of slavery?

Scholars and activists concerned with the Afterlives of Atlantic World slavery do not speak as one on the question of what is to be done. Indeed, some do not believe the problems they identify can be remedied. In the US, thinkers in the philosophical school described as "Afro-pessimism" argue that through Atlantic World slavery, the distinction between the Human and the Slave was racialised, such that the categories of Slave and Black became interchangeable, and it is this, not simply oppression or exploitation, that defines the Black condition. Anti-Blackness thus represents a unique challenge to liberal societies that no reform can address, since liberalism promises to free humanity, but to be Black is to be excluded from the realm of the human. However, other Afterlives thinkers do see possibilities for political action to address the living legacies of Atlantic World slavery. They struggle, among other things, for reparatory and racial justice, for the defunding of militarised policing and border controls, and against the prison industrial complex and the forms of criminalisation and exclusion that create the populations it cages.

As with all political efforts to extend human freedom and flourishing, there are divisions between those who advocate a more gradual, reformist approach and those who call for immediate, revolutionary change; as well as between those who limit their concern to transforming conditions for specific groups within particular nations, and those who seek universal rights and global transformation. The details of the recommendations for action that spring from Afterlives thinking are therefore the focus of debate. Nonetheless, I believe that Afterlives scholarship identifies the general direction in which we need to travel both to address the limitations of measures advocated by contemporary antislavery NGOs, and to counter the ongoing harms set in train by the history of Atlantic World slavery.

Reparations and reparatory justice

The term "reparations" refers to repairing a wrong or injury, making atonement, and repaying debts, often including compensation in money and land. It was historically used mainly to refer to payments made by states vanquished in war to compensate for damage wrought in other states, but has been extended to cover calls for compensation for groups injured by other state actions. In 1952, Germany agreed to pay US$927 million to Holocaust survivors; in 2013, the British government agreed to pay almost £20 million in compensation to Kenyan claimants for atrocities against the Mau Mau freedom fighters committed by Britain's colonial administration; in 2021, Germany agreed to pay Namibia around £940m in recognition of the Herero-Nama genocide at the start of the 20th century. Such compensation payments are rare, and are usually described as acts of reconciliation, not reparation.

The idea that states and private individuals who benefitted from slavery are morally obligated to make restitution to those violated by it is not new. In an autobiography written in 1787, Ottobah Cugoano (1999 [1787]), who was born in what is now Ghana but captured as a child and sold into slavery in the Caribbean, made a powerful case for reparations to African societies harmed by the slave trade. Demands for some form of compensation for victims of slave trading and slavery have continued to be articulated since then. Today's movement for slavery reparations includes an array of activists, scholars, attorneys, and legislators whose thinking on the issue and proposed policy solutions varies widely (Bhabha et al., 2021).

For obvious reasons, the idea of slavery reparations is vociferously opposed by white supremacists. But others also reject it on grounds that so much time has passed since the abolition of slavery that if contemporary taxpayers were compelled to foot the bill to atone for crimes committed by people long since dead it would create a new and different injustice. Yet there are historical precedents for taxpayers funding reparations for actions taken long ago and for which they bear no personal responsibility. In 1825, in exchange for recognising Haiti's independence, France demanded 150 million francs which the French state would use for compensation payments to almost 8,000 former slave owners and their descendants. To finance these vast "reparations", Haiti was forced to borrow from French banks, and the interests and fees on the loans added to the country's debt to France. Repayments on this debt continued until 1947, long after the original slaveholders were all dead (Craemer, 2021). And as already noted, until 2015, UK taxpayers continued to service government debt for compensation payments to slave owners. If the passage of time did not undo governments' legal responsibility to honour debts incurred to compensate slave owners and their descendants, why should it cancel their obligation to compensate the enslaved and their descendants?

In addition to calls for states to make reparations, there are activists who demand reparations from other direct beneficiaries of slavery, such as universities that were endowed funds by people whose wealth derived from slavery. A number of US universities, and in the UK, the University of Glasgow, have now committed to some form of reparatory justice. The question of what form reparations should take is much debated. Some activism is narrowly focused on securing direct financial compensation for individual descendants of enslaved people to compensate them for the theft of their forebears' labour, culture and humanity. However, other scholars and activists have reservations about whether a price tag can or should be placed on the degradation and suffering of slavery. How could any amount of mere money actually repair its harms, or restore what was stolen from those who were enslaved and from their descendants?

Another problem for proponents of reparations in the form of direct financial compensation to descendants of enslaved people is that there are people today racialised as white whose forebears were enslaved Africans.

In Brazil, this has already had implications for efforts to address racial inequalities through forms of affirmative action. Fewer people self-identified as white in the 2020 census than had done so in the 2010 census. Some attribute this to growing levels of education and racial consciousness leading to greater pride in African ancestry amongst *pardo* Brazilians. But others suspect that formerly "white" people often have more cynical motives. For example, in 2020, the Brazilian electoral court ruled that government resources granted to political parties must be split proportionately between its white and non-white candidates. In the city council and mayoral elections that followed, more than 42,000 politicians who ran for office changed their self-declared racialised identity from white to Afro-Brazilian (Janusz, 2021). If reparations were offered to all those with enslaved African ancestry, there is no doubt that the beneficiaries would include many thousands of Brazilians who have always identified as white and enjoyed the privileges of whiteness in Brazilian society.

Such difficulties are less pronounced where demands for reparations focus on repairing the collective, rather than individual, damage wrought by slavery and its aftermaths. In Brazil, some reparations activism has centred on securing land and rights for excluded and impoverished communities, members of which are mostly but not exclusively racialised as Black, *pardo* or indigenous. In 1988, the new Brazilian Constitution deemed that the rural communities descended from runaway slaves, known as *quilombos*, could be officially recognised and granted collective title to their lands. Some Black social movements saw the potential for reparatory justice through recognition as *quilombos*. In 2003, the Lula administration decreed that any community that self-identified as Afro-Brazilian, even those living in urban neighbourhoods, could apply for the status of *quilombo* and receive a collective land deed. By 2017, more than 2,000 communities had been officially recognised as such, and around 10 per cent of them had been issued with land titles. The government had also started to provide *quilombo* communities with a package of social and welfare rights, including education, housing, and food security.

In the US too, calls for reparations are often articulated as demands for measures that target the structural inequalities experienced by Black Americans *per se*, such as a national fund to create economic and educational opportunities for Black communities, and/or for measures to redistribute wealth and land ownership. The Caribbean's CARICOM Reparations Commission (CRC) provides another example of the kind of claims that can be made for collective, rather than individual, restitution. The CRC observes that European governments, as well as private individuals, owned and traded enslaved Africans, and that as well as destroying indigenous communities in the Caribbean, they created the legal and financial structures that made the enslavement of Africans possible. To this day, these governments have refused to acknowledge crimes perpetrated to advance their own "national interests" or to seek ways in which to repair the lasting damage of these crimes.

The CRC identifies a comprehensive programme as the path to reconciliation, truth and justice for victims and their descendants. That programme includes calls to establish cultural and research institutions in the region to inform and educate local populations about the crimes of colonialism and slavery, to fund measures to address the public health crisis of the region and to eradicate illiteracy. It also notes that the heavy debts carried by governments in the Caribbean region properly belong to the former colonial powers, and argues that support for the payment of domestic debt and cancellation of international debt are necessary reparatory actions.

Debt cancellation, land rights, and investment in public health, education, and welfare primarily targeting populations racialised as Black in the US, Brazil and the Caribbean would all do much to reduce the numbers of people who have no choice but to accept the kind of work that is associated with labour and human rights abuses, as would the same kind of reparatory measures in former European and US colonies elsewhere in the world. Supporting movements for reparatory justice is therefore a way in which we can simultaneously address the Afterlives of slavery and colonialism, and the conditions that create vulnerability to exploitation and violence described by antislavery NGOs as "modern slavery".

Important as such measures are, reparations (in whatever form they take) are not a "silver bullet" solution to the problems discussed in this book. Gains secured through reparations activism can be lost. This is illustrated by the fact that under the right-wing administration of Bolsonaro, *quilombo* communities are finding it ever harder to defend their land rights in the face of aggressive, sometimes murderously violent, land grabs that are tacitly (or not so tacitly) condoned by the authorities. Moreover, if the racial and national logics that currently order global capitalism remain intact, reparations will not bring about sustainable changes, no matter what form they take. The pursuit of reparatory justice has to be part of a much wider global political movement, including struggles for free movement and migrants' rights.

No borders!

In the US in the nineteenth century, struggles against Fugitive Slave laws and other restrictions on the mobility of free Black people helped to consolidate an understanding of freedom of movement as central to personal liberty. The denial of what Frederick Douglass (a nineteenth century US intellectual who had himself escaped slavery) termed the "right of locomotion" was a central feature of enslavement, and a crucial component of freedom (Roberts, 2018). Pursuing this right is another way in which to simultaneously address the ongoing wrongs of slavery and colonialism and reduce the incidence of many of the phenomena described by antislavery NGOs as "modern slavery".

Without borders and visa requirements, for example, the many thousands of Nigerian, Ghanaian and other sub-Saharan African asylum seekers and migrants who have been brutally exploited and tortured in Libya could have flown directly to Europe, while escapees from Eritrea and South Sudan could have made their way to Egypt and boarded one of the no-frills flights that cheaply and safely transport European holiday makers across the Mediterranean. Without borders, there would be no market for the mobility services (both legal and criminalised) that generate debts and dependencies of a type that sometimes lead to abuse and exploitation. Migrants would no longer provide a pool of hyper-exploitable labour, or have to fear that reporting violence, rape or wage theft by an abusive recruiter or employer would lead to their own deportation.

People will not stop moving, especially given climate change, the foreign policies of global north that create political instability in global south, the economic policies that undermine global south economies and welfare systems, and in the case of Africa, the fact the continent has a growing youthful population with restricted employment opportunities. The current regime of national state control over human mobility is designed for the purpose of excluding these unwanted people (Sharma, 2020), and has developed a global and extremely violent system of militarised borders, deportations and removals, refugee and internment camps, and detention centres and prison islands where the rights, freedoms, and dignity of "unwanted" human beings are routinely and horribly violated.

As Harsha Walia (2021) argues, borders are the product of histories of violent territorial expansion, settler-colonialism, slavery, and gendered racial exclusion, and are today operated to maintain a form of neo-colonial, global apartheid. It is the movement of people from global south countries who have been impoverished by histories of slavery, colonialism and empire that is most heavily and systematically constrained by the current system of national-state control over human mobility. Eliminating those restraints on movement is one extremely important means by which global north nations enriched by slavery, colonial rule, and imperial ventures can make reparations.

For many decades, mainstream political parties in global north countries have either actively stoked, or failed to challenge, anti-immigrant sentiment, so calls for border abolition are unlikely to be popular. Yet calls for the abolition of the slave trade and slavery were equally unpopular in Europe and the Americas in the past. The reasons given by those who oppose border abolition today are remarkably similar to objections voiced by those who opposed slavery's abolition in the past. Universal enjoyment of the right of locomotion and full and equal rights for global south migrants in global north countries would threaten the economies and social fabric of the latter, they say.

People from the global south are assumed to lack the qualities and attributes that would allow them to integrate into modern liberal societies. "They" are criminals and rapists; "they" don't value families or respect women as "we" do; "they" don't understand democracy. "They" are lazy and dependent scroungers, although "they" will also steal "our" jobs and depress wages. Exactly the same fears were voiced by many white and free citizens in the US, Brazil and European colonies when the move towards abolition confronted them with the spectre of former slaves being incorporated into their societies as equal citizens.

To call for the abolition of all immigration controls, amnesty for those without official documents and equal rights regardless of nationality is often seen as too radical to even contemplate. But it is worth remembering that calling for an end to the legal and social border between free persons and slaves was once seen as an equally impossible and unrealistic dream. Again, however, the abolition of borders is not enough, on its own, to address all the injustices and inequalities described in this book.

Abolition democracy: Prisons and police

In his 1935 book, *Black Reconstruction in America,* W.E.B Du Bois used the term "abolition-democracy" to describe the political movement required to dismantle the legal, social, economic and political mechanisms through which the racialised power relations of slavery were maintained in the post-abolition US. The criminal justice system was amongst those he identified as perpetuating racial domination, an argument that carries equal weight today, given the vast racial disparities in terms of who falls victim to police violence as well as in sentencing practices and rates of incarceration.

Partly inspired by Du Bois' work, demands for prisons to be abolished were subsequently articulated by left leaning thinkers such as Angela Davis (2003), who argues that prisons are obsolete institutions that exacerbate rather than moderate or solve social harms, and that we need a justice system based on reparation and reconciliation rather than retribution and vengeance. Today, there is a global movement for prison abolition. It has no structured organizing or leadership group, but is formed by a collection of individuals and groups seeking to transform the ways in which crime is imagined and dealt with.

Prison abolitionists identify three steps that need to be taken. First, an immediate moratorium on the building of prisons and immigration detention facilities. Second, initiate a programme of decarceration, which should begin with the release of those prisoners who represent no threat to society, for example, those serving sentences for nonviolent crimes and those caged in prisons or immigration detention centres charged with or convicted of entry-related offenses or non-compliance with some element of their visas. Third, develop excarceration strategies. The abolition of border controls, and the decriminalisation of drug use and of sex work, are very obvious ways to begin to stem the flow of people into prisons and detention facilities. Around the world, people who are experiencing mental health crises are also extremely vulnerable to criminalisation and incarceration, so funding mental health services and ensuring that mental health professionals, not police, are first-responders to mental health related crises represents another important excarceration strategy.

In the wake of George Floyd's murder, and the continuing stream of police slayings of unarmed Black people since, protesters have often carried placards reading "abolish the police" or "defund the police". Patrisse

Cullors, co-founder of the BLM movement, explains that such slogans are shorthand for a call to reduce the resources available for law enforcement to harm Black people and redirect those funds into redressing histories of racial injustice and exclusion by investing in social services for mental health, domestic violence and homelessness, as well as schools, hospitals, housing and food, in predominantly Black neighbourhoods. Such proposals can hardly be rejected on grounds of costs. The US annually spends some $80 billion on "correctional" institutions. To this we should add the massive social and financial costs borne by incarcerated persons, families, children, and communities.

In Brazil, too, longstanding demands for the demilitarisation of the police are starting to be accompanied by calls for the abolition of police and prisons altogether, with the revenues saved being redirected into social spending. In the US, such calls have actually gained some traction in policy circles. Some cities have divested from police budgets in order to be able to reallocate funds to the kind of programmes activists advocate. In Portland, Oregon, two teams that had been accused of over-policing Black communities have been disbanded; in San Francisco, city officials have agreed to divert $120 million from policing into health programmes and workforce training, and in Minneapolis, cuts to the police budget are being used to develop a mental health team to respond to 911 calls linked to mental health crises. Similar moves are planned or underway in some other cities.

Yet calls for police defunding or abolition, rather than reform, are not unanimously welcomed even by people racialised as Black in the US, not least because violent crime remains a serious threat, especially to the lives and wellbeing of poorer people. Some are also concerned that demands for police abolition grounded in a vision of a wider transformation of social and political relations could be subverted to further a very different, neoliberal agenda, in which cuts to criminal justice systems are not accompanied by increased spending on any other public services.

This anxiety reminds us that actions against single elements of the interwoven systems of domination set in train by slavery and colonialism are not enough to prevent people from being swept up in their wake (Sharpe, 2016). Struggles to transform criminal justice systems and policing, and against borders, and for reparations and wealth redistribution are indivisible (Gilmore Wilson, 2022).

conclusion

Slavery has been identified as a serious current problem in the twenty-first century by actors concerned with two apparently separate sets of violence and injustice – "modern slavery" and the "Afterlives of Atlantic World slavery". And yet, as I hope this book has shown, the forms of violence, exploitation and injustice discussed under the heading "modern slavery" are not unrelated to histories of slavery and colonialism. Populations that are today vulnerable to extreme forms of labour abuse, to exploitation and abuse in the course of migration, and to other forms of predation by unscrupulous or violent individuals, have been made so by these histories and the economic, social, and political inequalities they set in train. It is overwhelmingly people who are racialised as Black, brown or "other" who are at the sharp end of these processes.

The campaign against "modern slavery" is highly selective about the forms of violence, exploitation and injustice it recognises and seeks to eliminate. Antislavery actors call for outrage and immediate action in relation to the child domestic worker who is caged, beaten and degraded by an employer, the woman who is raped by a brothel keeper, the person who is held at gunpoint in a remote logging camp, the migrant who dies at the hands of a trafficker. They do not demand the same outrage or action in relation to the far greater numbers of children separated from their families and caged in immigration detention centres, women raped by border guards and police officers, people held at gunpoint in makeshift camps at Europe's borders, migrants who die as a result of push back operations, and so on. Individual antislavery actors may well think these forms of state-sponsored violence are very wrong, but nonetheless imagine them as extrinsic to the criminal violence of "modern slavery", which they regard as a more urgent problem. This is an analysis that lets states off the hook.

Worse still, antislavery NGOs' analysis allows politicians to engage in a form of doublespeak whereby border policies that strip people of dignity and rights, render them vulnerable to violence and exploitation, and even kill them, are presented as measures to defend them from the evil of trafficking and "modern slavery". The fact that during her period as Home Secretary, Theresa May both introduced the UK's Modern Slavery Bill and viciously enforced "hostile environment" policies that led, among other harms, to the Windrush scandal, is one illustration of the hypocrisy that is made possible by detaching concerns about "modern slavery" from concerns about the "Afterlives of slavery". Current Home Secretary, Priti Patel, continues the tradition, condemning "modern slavery" while organising mass deportations to Jamaica, for instance. Patel also engages in dog whistle racism by claiming that those crossing the Channel in small boats are brought by "criminal gangs" of traffickers and smugglers who "laugh in the face of the British people" (Conservatives, 2020), while at the same time herself presiding over cruel and often unlawful deportations of asylum seekers.

More generally, the movement against "modern slavery" has only secured the backing of powerful political and business elites because antislavery NGOs make politically neutral demands that pose no threat to the existing status quo. The powerful can meet their calls by simply doing more of the same – criminalising the survival strategies of the poor, militarising borders to keep the unwanted out, encouraging TNCs to monitor their own activities, but not holding them legally responsible for their failures, requiring them to recognise and negotiate with unions, or even forcing them to pay tax.

By contrast, the Afterlives perspective generates calls for reparations, border abolition, and fundamental changes to criminal justice systems, calls that find little favour amongst privileged elites. None of these measures would be enough on their own. Even if reparations activism led to significant sums being invested in poor Black communities in the US and Brazil, or being secured by Caribbean governments from former colonial powers, there is no guarantee of their long-term impact if the racial and national logics that currently order global capitalism remain in place.

It is not possible to repair damage or atone for sins that are ongoing. The problem is not simply that in the past, rich industrialised countries became rich and industrialised by extracting resources from the global south, and dispossessing, exterminating and/or enslaving its peoples. It is that the global north continues to extract wealth from the global south in the form of raw materials and human labour power.

Likewise, though the abolition of borders is a vital part of dismantling the economic, political and social Afterlives of slavery and colonialism, and should be envisaged as a form of reparatory justice, it is not enough. Freedom of locomotion is a very partial and limited freedom if all it grants is the liberty to undertake poorly paid work and experience racism in a different country. By the same token, even the most radical reforms of prisons and policing are not sufficient. "Abolition democracy" as envisaged by Du Bois and Davis can never be achieved through standalone actions against singular manifestations of injustice. In the same way that the abolition of slavery as a legal status was a necessary, but not sufficient, move in the struggle for enslaved people's equality and freedom, so the dismantling of any one individual element of the system of racial domination spawned by slavery will not be enough to truly liberate their descendants (or other marginalised and exploited groups).

Abolition democracy also requires reparatory global justice and wealth redistribution, and fundamental and global changes to the ways in which production and consumption are organised, as well as to the ways in which care (for children, the elderly, the disabled, those with mental health problems, etc.) is imagined and organised, and an end to gendered hierarchies. Antislavery actors might say that this is a project so huge as to take us well beyond a concern with slavery. Yet the problems they dub "modern slavery" are so completely enmeshed in these wider structural inequalities and hierarchies as to be impossible to remedy without engaging in a larger political struggle for freedom and equality. One thing that the history of slavery's abolition teaches us is that freedom is not simply release from legal bondage, nor is it a "thing" that the powerful can kindly bestow upon a lowly class while firmly keeping the structures that position them as powerful and subaltern groups as lowly in place.

To the extent that today's antislavery actors attempt to hold states to their existing obligations under international law, we can say that the world they pursue is a better one than the one we currently live in. But those who wish to overcome domination in all its guises need to look well beyond anything that antislavery NGOs currently ask for. We have to keep thinking about what reparatory justice for slavery and colonialism would look like, keep trying to imagine and strive for a borderless world, a world in which whiteness, maleness and heterosexuality no longer mark special and particular privileges, a world in which labour and land are decommodified and a truly human and sustainable global economy established.

acknowledgements

I am extremely grateful to Series Editor Chris Grey and to my colleague Angelo Martins Junior for their encouragement and extremely helpful comments on drafts of this book.

further reading

The literature on the history of slavery and abolition is so vast that it's difficult to select a handful of key texts. However, the following address various different aspects of that history in different parts of the Atlantic world, and are highly recommended:

Blackett, R. (2018) *The Captive's Quest for Freedom: Fugitive Slaves, the 1850 Slave Law and the Politics of Slavery*. Cambridge: Cambridge University Press.

Brown V. (2010) *The Reaper's Garden*. Cambridge, MA: Harvard University Press.

Camp, S. (2004) *Closer to Freedom: Enslaved Women and Everyday Resistance in the Plantation South*. London: University of North Carolina Press.

Du Bois, W.E.B. (1935) *Black Reconstruction in America: 1860–1880*. New York, NY: Free Press.

Hartman, S. (2007) *Lose Your Mother: A Journey Along the Atlantic Slave Route*. New York, NY: Farrar, Straus and Giroux.

Rediker, M. (2008) *The Slave Ship: A Human History*. London: John Murray.

Reis, J. (2015) *Divining Slavery and Freedom: The Story of Domingos Sodré, an African Priest in Nineteenth-Century Brazil*. Cambridge, MA: Cambridge University Press.

Scott, R. (ed.) (1988) *The Abolition Of Slavery And The Aftermath Of Emancipation In Brazil*. Durham: Duke University Press.

Williams, E. (1984) *From Columbus to Castro: The History of the Caribbean 1492–1969*. London: Vintage.

The website of the Centre for the Study of the Legacies of British Slavery at University College London also provides links to a wealth of very accessible resources: www.ucl.ac.uk/lbs/

For those interested in debates on racial capitalism, Gargi Bhattacharya's (2018), *Rethinking Racial Capitalism: Questions of Reproduction and Survival* (London and New York: Rowman and Littlefield) and Ruth Gilmore Wilson's (2022) *Change Everything: Racial Capitalism and the Case for Abolition* (Chicago: Haymarket) would be excellent places to start, while those interested in slavery's place in the history of political thought will find Laura Brace's (2019) *The Politics of Slavery* (Edinburgh: University of Edinburgh Press) illuminating. To pursue questions about how the violence of racial slavery reaches into injustices and inequalities in the present, I recommend:

Alexander, M. (2010) *The New Jim Crow: Mass Incarceration in the Age of Colorblindness*. New York, NY: The New Press.

Berger, G. and Nunes, Z. (eds) (2019) *The Plantation, the Postplantation, and the Afterlives of Slavery*. Durham, NC: Duke University Press.

De Noronha, L. (2020) *Deporting Black Britons: Portraits of Deportation to Jamaica*. Manchester: Manchester University Press.

Miles, T. (2019) *Race and Afro-Brazilian Agency in Brazil*. London: Routledge.

Thomas, D. (2011) *Exceptional Violence: Embodied Citizenship in Transnational Jamaica*. Durham, NC: Duke University Press.

For readings on reparations, I would suggest Hilary Beckles' (2013) *Britain's Black Debt: Reparations for Caribbean Slavery and Native Genocide* (Kingston: University of the West Indies Press); Ta-Nehisi Coates' (2014) article, 'The Case for Reparations' in *The Atlantic* (www.theatlantic.com/magazin e/archive/2014/06/the-case-for-reparations/361631/ [accessed December 13, 2021]); and the collection edited by Bhabha, Matache and Elkins (2021) *Time for Reparations* (Philadelphia, PA: University of Pennsylvania Press).

The literature on the violence and injustice of borders and immigration regimes is again huge, but Nandita Sharma's (2020) *Home Rule: National Sovereignty and the Separation of Natives and Migrants* (Durham, NC: Duke University Press) provides a brilliant insight into their history and a powerful critique of nation-state sovereignty. Other suggestions are:

Bhatia, M. and Canning, V. (eds) (2021) *Stealing Time: Migration, Temporalities and State Violence*. London: Palgrave Macmillan.

King, N. (2016) *No Borders: The Politics of Immigration Control and Resistance*. London: Zed.

Sanchez, G. (2015) *Human Smuggling and Border Crossings*. London: Routledge.

For further reading on "modern slavery", see Emily Kenway's (2021) *The Truth About Modern Slavery* (London: Pluto) and openDemocracy's *Beyond Trafficking & Slavery* platform, which features an abundance of very accessible short articles and ebooks based on the latest academic research on contemporary phenomena that antislavery NGOs describe as "modern slavery" – www.opendemocracy.net/en/beyond-trafficking-and-slavery/ (accessed December 13, 2021).

references

Amnesty International (2016a) 'Amnesty International publishes policy and research on protection of sex workers' rights', *Amnesty International,* May 26. www.amnesty.org/en/latest/news/2016/05/amnesty-international-publishes-policy-and-research-on-protection-of-sex-workers-rights/ (accessed December 13, 2021).

Amnesty International (2016b) *Waiting in Vain: Unlawful police killings and relatives' long struggle for justice.* Amnesty International. Available from www.amnesty.org/en/documents/amr38/5092/2016/en/ (accessed December 13, 2021).

Amnesty International (2021) 'Why the police crackdown makes racism worse', Campaigns Blog, Amnesty International UK, June 30. www.amnesty.org.uk/blogs/campaigns-blog/why-police-crackdown-bill-makes-racism-worse?from=issue (accessed January 19 2022).

Anderson, B. (2013) *Us and Them: The Dangerous Politics of Immigration Control.* Oxford: Oxford University Press.

Andersson, R. (2014) *Illegality, Inc.* Oakland, CA: University of California Press.

Archer, N., Torrisi, C., Provost, C., Nabert, A. and Lobos, B. (2019) 'Hundreds of Europeans 'criminalised' for helping migrants', *openDemocracy,* May 18. www.opendemocracy.net/en/5050/hundreds-of-europeans-criminalised-for-helping-migrants-new-data-shows-as-far-right-aims-to-win-big-in-european-elections/ (accessed January 6 2022).

ASI (2015) *Forced Labour in the Brick Kiln Sector in India.* London: Antislavery International. www.antislavery.org/wp-content/uploads/2017/01/forced-labour-in-brick-kilns-in-india-august-2015-briefing.pdf (accessed January 6 2022).

Bales, K. (2010) *'How to combat modern slavery',* TedX, www.ted.com/talks/kevin_bales_how_to_combat_modern_slavery (accessed January 6 2022).

Bales, K. and Soodalter, R. (2009) *The Slave Next Door.* Berkeley, CA: University of California Press.

Betterlivesleeds (2016) 'Trust your instinct – be part of the World Day against Human Trafficking', *Better Lives for People in Leeds.* August 1. https://betterlivesleeds.wordpress.com/2016/08/01/trust-your-instinct-be-part-of-world-day-against-human-trafficking/ (accessed December 13 2021).

Bhabha, J., Matache, M. and Elkins, C. (eds) (2021) *Time for Reparations*. Philadelphia, PA: University of Pennsylvania Press.

Border Violence Monitoring Network (2021) *Annual Torture Report 2020*, BVMN. Available from www.borderviolence.eu/annual-torture-report-2020/ (accessed December 13 2021).

Bourne, G. (1845) *A Condensed Anti-Slavery Bible Argument: By a Citizen of Virginia*. New York, NY: S. W. Benedict. http://docsouth.unc.edu/church/bourne/bourne.html (accessed December 13 2021).

Chalhoub, S. (2006) 'The politics of silence: Race and citizenship in nineteenth-century Brazil', *Slavery & Abolition*, 27 (1): 73–87.

Childs, D. (2015) *Slaves of the State: Black Incarceration from the Chain Gang to the Penitentiary*. Minneapolis, MN: University of Minnesota Press.

Chung, J. (2021) 'Voting rights in the era of mass incarceration: A primer', *The Sentencing Project*. www.sentencingproject.org/publications/felony-disenfranchisement-a-primer/ (accessed December 13 2021).

Conservatives (2020) 'Priti Patel: Fixing our broken asylum system', *Conservatives.com,* October 4. www.conservatives.com/news/2020/priti-patel–fixing-our-broken-asylum-system (accessed December 13 2021).

Corporate Watch (2019) 'A life costs £10,000: How G4S' Brook House detention contract works'. *Corporate Watch,* July 24. https://corporatewatch.org/a-life-costs-10000-how-g4s-brook-house-detention-contract-works/ (accessed December 13 2021).

Craemer, T. (2021) 'There was a time reparations were actually paid out – just not to formerly enslaved people', *The Conversation*, February 26. https://theconversation.com/there-was-a-time-reparations-were-actually-paid-out-just-not-to-formerly-enslaved-people-152522 (accessed December 13 2021).

Crenshaw, K., Gotanda, N., Peller, G. and Thomas, K. (1996) *Critical Race Theory: The Key Writings That Formed the Movement*. New York, NY: The New Press.

Cugoano, O. (1999 [1787]) *Thoughts and Sentiments on the Evil and Wicked Traffic of the Human Species*. London: Penguin Classics.

Davis, A. (2003) *Are Prisons Obsolete?* New York, NY: Seven Stories Press.

De Noronha, L. (2020) *Deporting Black Britons: Portraits of Deportation to Jamaica*. Manchester: Manchester University Press.

Du Bois, W.E.B. (1935) *Black Reconstruction in America: 1860–1880*. New York, NY: Free Press.

Eltis, D. (2018) 'Trans-Atlantic Slave Trade – Understanding the Database: Methodology', *Slave Voyages*. www.slavevoyages.org/voyage/about#methodology/introduction/0/en/ (accessed December 13 2021).

ETUC (2021) 'Huge fall in labour inspections raises Covid risk', *Syndicat European Trade Union*, April 28. www.etuc.org/en/pressrelease/huge-fall-labour-inspections-raises-covid-risk (accessed December 13 2021).

Fair Labor Association (2018) *Triple Discrimination: Woman, Pregnant, and Migrant*. Available from www.fairlabor.org/report/triple-discrimination-woman-pregnant-and-migrant (accessed December 13 2021).

GBD 2019 Police Violence US Subnational Collaborators (2021) 'Fatal police violence by state in the USA, 1980–2019', *The Lancet*, 398 (10307): 1239–55.

Gilmore Wilson, R. (2022) *Change Everything: Racial Capitalism and the Case for Abolition*. Chicago, IL: Haymarket.

Hartman, S. (2007) *Lose Your Mother: A Journey Along the Atlantic Slave Route*. New York, NY: Farrar, Straus and Giroux.

Hickel, J., Sullivan, D. and Zoomkawala, H. (2021) 'Plunder in the post-colonial era: Quantifying drain from the global south through unequal exchange, 1960–2018', *New Political Economy*, 26 (6): 1030–47.

Human Rights Watch (2021) '"Everything I have to do is tied to a man": Women and Qatar's male guardianship rules', *HRW*. www.hrw.org/report/2021/03/29/everything-i-have-do-tied-man/women-and-qatars-male-guardianship-rules (accessed December 13 2021).

ILO (2013) *Employment Practices and Working Conditions in Thailand's Fishing Sector*. Geneva: International Labour Office.

IMF (2021) *Measuring the Informal Economy*. Washington, DC: International Monetary Fund. Available from www.imf.org/en/Publications/Policy-Papers/Issues/2021/02/02/Measuring-the-Informal-Economy-50057 (accessed December 13 2021).

IOM (2019) *Migrants and their Vulnerability to Human Trafficking, Modern Slavery and Forced Labour*. Geneva: International Organisation for Migration. Available from https://publications.iom.int/books/migrants-and-their-vulnerability-human-trafficking-modern-slavery-and-forced-labour (accessed December 13 2021).

Jaffe, R. and Diphoorn, T. (2019) 'Old Boys and Badmen: Private Security in (Post)Colonial Jamaica', *Interventions*, 21 (7): 909–27.

Janusz, A. (2021) 'Thousands of Brazilians who won elections as black candidates in 2020 previously ran for office as white', *SBS News*, January 12. www.sbs.com.au/news/dateline/thousands-of-brazilians-who-won-elections-as-black-candidates-in-2020-previously-ran-for-office-as-white (accessed December 13 2021).

Justice & Care (2018) 'About Us', *Justice & Care*. https://justiceandcare.org/about-us/ (accessed December 13 2021).

Kempadoo, K., Sanghera, J. and Pattanaik, B. (eds) (2005) *Trafficking and Prostitution Reconsidered*. London: Paradigm.

Kendi, I. (2016) *Stamped from the Beginning*. New York, NY: Nation Books.

Keo, C. (2013) *Human Trafficking in Cambodia*. London: Routledge.

Kristine, L. (2012) 'Photos that bear witness to modern slavery', *TEDx*, January www.ted.com/talks/lisa_kristine_photos_that_bear_witness_to_modern_slavery?language=en?

LeBaron, G. (2020) *Combatting Modern Slavery: Why Labour Governance is Failing and What We Can Do About It*. Cambridge: Polity.

Mai, N. (2018) *Mobile Orientations*. Chicago, IL: University of Chicago Press.

Mills, C. (1997) *The Racial Contract*. Ithaka, NY: Cornell University Press.

Missing Migrants Project (2021) 'Missing Migrants Project', *International Organisation for Migration*. https://gmdac.iom.int/missing-migrants-project-0 (accessed December 13, 2021).

Muñoz, C. (2020) 'Brazil suffers its own scourge of police brutality', *Human Rights Watch*, June 3. www.hrw.org/news/2020/06/03/brazil-suffers-its-own-scourge-police-brutality (accessed December 13 2021).

O'Connell Davidson, J. (2015) *Modern Slavery and the Margins of Freedom*. London: Palgrave.

Okyere, S., Agyeman, N. and Saboro, E. (2021). '"Why Was He Videoing Us?": The ethics and politics of audio-visual propaganda in child trafficking and human trafficking campaigns', *Anti-Trafficking Review*, 16: 47–68.

Oxfam (2019) 'The People Behind the Prices', *Oxfam Briefing Paper*, February. https://oxfamilibrary.openrepository.com/bitstream/10546/620619/2/rr-people-behind-prices-tomato-060219-summ-en.pdf (accessed December 13 2021).

Patterson, O. (1982) *Slavery and Social Death*. Cambridge, MA: Harvard University Press.

Pattisson, P. (2021) 'G4S migrant workers "forced to pay millions" in illegal fees for jobs', *The Guardian*, January 18. www.theguardian.com/global-development/2021/jan/18/g4s-migrant-workers-forced-to-pay-millions-in-fees-for-jobs (accessed December 13 2021).

Pattison, P. and McIntyre, N. (2021) 'Revealed: 6,500 migrant workers have died in Qatar since World Cup awarded', *The Guardian*, February 23. www.theguardian.com/global-development/2021/feb/23/revealed-migrant-worker-deaths-qatar-fifa-world-cup-2022 (accessed December 13 2021).

Pollock, A. (2021) *Sickening Anti-Black Racism and Health Disparities in the United States*. Minneapolis, MN: University of Minnesota Press.

Prison Reform Trust (2019) *Prison: The Facts. Bromley Briefings, Summer*. www.prisonreformtrust.org.uk/Portals/0/Documents/Bromley%20Briefings/Prison%20the%20facts%20Summer%202019.pdf (accessed December 13 2021).

Roberts, N. (2018) *A Political Companion to Frederick Douglass*. Lexington: University of Kentucky Press.

Rosenthal, C. (2018) *Accounting for Slavery: Masters and Management*. Harvard: Harvard University Press.

Sanchez, G. (2015) *Human Smuggling and Border Crossings*. London: Routledge.

Schafer, D. (2018) *Anna Madgigine Jai Kingsley: African Princess, Florida Slave, Plantation Slaveholder*. Gainesville, FL: University Press of Florida.

Sharma, N. (2020) *Home Rule: National Sovereignty and the Separation of Natives and Migrants*. Durham, NC: Duke University Press.

Sharpe, C. (2016) *In the Wake: On Blackness and Being*. Durham, NC: Duke University Press.

Skilbrei, M. and Spanger, M. (2019) *Understanding Sex for Sale: Meanings and Moralities of Sexual Commerce*. London: Routledge.

Swift, J. (2018) 'Afro-Brazilians and contemporary lynchings in Brazil', *Black Perspectives (AAIHS)*, April 19. www.aaihs.org/afro-brazilians-and-contemporary-lynchings-in-brazil/ (accessed December 13 2021).

Tondo, L. (2021) *'Revealed: 2.000 refugee deaths linked to illegal EU pushbacks'*, Guardian, May 5. www.theguardian.com/global-development/2021/may/05/revealed-2000-refugee-deaths-linked-to-eu-pushbacks (accessed January 6 2022).

Tradehub (2019) 'Novel study maps out the inequality of land distribution and ownership in Brazil', *Trade, Development & the Environment Hub*. https://tradehub.earth/2020/08/10/novel-study-maps-out-the-inequality-of-land-distribution-and-ownership-in-brazil/ (accessed January 6 2022).

UCL (2022) *Legacies of Slavery, University College London Department of History*. www.ucl.ac.uk/lbs/ (accessed January 6 2022).

Unchecked (2020) 'Cuts are making it harder to enforce the rules that stop exploitation'. *Unchecked UK*. https://unchecked.uk/the-issues/where-we-work/ (accessed December 13 2021).

UNITED (2020) 'Updated Refugee Death List 2020', *United for Intercultural Action*. www.unitedagainstracism.org/blog/2020/06/19/updated-refugee-death-list-2020/ (accessed December 13 2021).

Walia, H. (2021) *Border Rule*. Chicago, IL: Haymarket.

Walters, K. (2019) 'End the system of forced rescue and institutionalisation in India', *Beyond Trafficking and Slavery*, openDemocracy, January 8. www.opendemocracy.net/en/beyond-trafficking-and-slavery/end-system-of-forced-rescue-and-institutionalisation-in-india/ (accessed December 13 2021).

World Bank (2020) *2020 State of the Artisanal and Small-Scale Mining Sector*. Washington, DC: World Bank. www.trafigura.com/media/3127/2020_trafigura_state_of_artisanal_and_small_scale_mining_sector_report.pdf (accessed December 13 2021).

index